JEFFREY ALLE[N]

SECRETS OF SINGING

CONSULTING EDITOR
Sandy Feldstein

PRODUCTION COORDINATOR
Diane Laucirica

DESIGN AND LAYOUT
Susan Hartline-Long

EDITED
by Cathy J. Moulton

INSTRUCTIONAL DRAWINGS
by Kimberley Allen

PHOTOGRAPHY
by Mitch Tobias

SOUND SOURCE
Engineered by David Feldstein

ON THE COVER
Photographed by Mitch Tobias
Artist: Peter Shambrook

Published by Warner Bros. Publications

To Kimberley,
Nicole and Jacqueline
who make my life sing...

Acknowledgements

A special thanks to Doris and Edward Allen, Lenore Cellini, Anthony Brienza, Lillian Kraus and Ben Wiener, without whom this book would probably never have been written.

I also wish to express gratitude to Mr. Herbert Allen and Mr. Henry Allen whose generous assistance was essential to the completion of this project.

I'm grateful to Dr. Sandy Feldstein for giving me the opportunity to write the book on singing I had in mind, and for showing great patience, offering first class support as well as invaluable advice along the way.

Very special thanks to my editor, assistant and friend, Cathy Moulton. Her expertise and steadfast dedication to this book were second to none.

Thanks always to Steve Grossman for his invaluable savvy and guidance regarding the writing business.

A heartfelt thank you to Natalie Limonic, whose tremendous musical sensitivity and unflinching passion for the vocal arts has been an inspiration to me for nearly two decades.

To all my teachers, especially Tom Dodson and Mr. and Mrs. Ernest Nadasi, who have enriched my life beyond measure.

Maro Donabedian deserves much appreciation for her expert assistance in the development of my musical endeavors.

Thank you to David Scott for apprising me of the serious nature of the vocal arts and getting me on the road that would take a lifetime to travel.

Cornelia "Chris" Korney deserves much recognition for teaching me that singing could open doors to the world at large and illuminate hidden talents within.

A big thanks to Anthony Allen for his initial contributions to the project and continued moral support.

Thanks to Sal Ferraro of Dimple's in Burbank, CA, for kindly lending the use of his facility for the live performance shots.

To all my photo models: Kristen Silver, LaLa, Peter Shambrook, Susan Hamilton, Raven Bushman, David Kaufman, Tracy Sutter, Evelyn Young, Paul Lacano, Paul Engel, Mark William Thompson, Amy Felmer, William Mikus, Denis Mandel, and Tony Garcia, thanks for your patience and for adding so much to this book.

Bravo to William Adams, Nancy Plochman, Tony Garcia and Kristen Silver who gave accomplished demonstrations of the exercises for the CDs accompanying this book.

And finally, applause to my students, past and present, for their dauntless quest to achieve success in the realm of their dreams...

To The Teacher

Secrets of Singing (SOS) is a powerful, yet readily accessible array of vocal techniques presented in direct and readable language. Students and teachers alike are invited to explore this inspiring, proven system that is suitable for all stylistic modes of vocal expression. Educational institutions, right up the line, from junior high school to junior college through four-year universities, colleges and extension levels can all benefit from this innovative program of vocal study.

SOS is designed to be flexible enough to accommodate the curricular demands of quarter or semester courses, as well as graduate or conservatory programs. The twelve chapters of Part One introduce the basic principles of singing. In Part Two, five chapters are dedicated to the upper voice -- its characteristics and mechanics. Part Three ties the foregoing chapters together with a discussion of the most prized vocal qualities of all -- an open throat and pleasing vibrato.

Part Four spotlights phrasing and the essential principles of singers' diction. The general reference chapters of Part Five are a great asset for teachers who need to find common ground for classes of disparate vocal types, styles, and levels. Students are challenged to think and "hear" for themselves via the chapters on "How to Practice" and the "Troubleshooting Guide".

For those classes sufficient in length and depth, Part Six contains a thorough, yet unusually accessible set of appendices which describe the vocal anatomy. Instructors can incorporate these addenda into their classroom study or assign them as homework or extra credit. A table of contents, detailed index, and handy glossary of common vocal terms are provided, allowing quick access to information in time-crucial classroom situations.

Accompanying the text, are dynamic exercises, visual aids, and two compact disks that make complex technical material clear and simple.The *SOS System* exercise disks ensure that students translate vocal concepts from mind to vocal muscles. In addition, there are three groups of unique endurance exercises gauged to meet the requirements of singers engaged in stage or studio work. With the *SOS System*, the classroom setting becomes an ideal training ground where students of singing can achieve a complete understanding of their vocal instrument.

TABLE OF CONTENTS

"The secret sits in the middle and knows, while others dance round in circles and suppose."

Robert Frost

PART ONE:

UNLEASHING YOUR VOCAL POWER

INTRODUCTION:
"SECRETS OF SINGING"

"Most singing is done not with the voice but with the ears and the brain."

Giuseppe DeLuca

SING BETTER NOW!

The practical information contained in this book will allow you to sing better immediately. Each section is worth months of private lessons. Though not meant to substitute for one-on-one lessons with a private instructor, the simplicity and practical nature of the advice will allow you to proceed in your own vocal development or pursue on-going lessons with greater confidence.

There are countless methods of singing. In fact, many teachers invent a singing system to suit their own vocal history and voice characteristics. Each method includes many different techniques, concepts and exercises. For the most part, many of the lessons given at voice studios involve repetition of unproductive exercises. Often, the only result of this work is painstakingly slow progress, if any.

Don't Get Caught in the Confusion

To make matters more complicated, libraries and bookstores contain an odd assortment of singing books. Many are old-fashioned and haven't aged well. Another group is written by doctors, and seemingly, for doctors since their language is so complex and confusing.

Even more frustrating is that the books written on singing contain information absolutely contradictory to each other. On one hand, an authoritative text says that strengthening the diaphragm is *the* key to success. The book down the shelf says that a study of diaphragm, breath control, etc., is simply a waste of time!

With the abundance of information floating around out there, you could spend a lifetime learning all the techniques offered as stepping stones to vocal freedom. Ironically, the basics that are the true foundation of vocal success are often lost amid this glut of information.

What you'll learn from *Secrets of Singing* is that *singing is simple.* It's actually kids' stuff when it's done right. Great vocal training is designed to remind you of how your voice worked when you were a child. The challenge is to combine a simple, yet powerful, technique with the passion of full-blown emotions. *Strong feelings will literally break down a voice not equipped with an equally sturdy technique.*

SETTING THE STAGE FOR EXPRESSIVE SINGING

This text is designed to be a clear and concise explanation of the technical side of singing. Technique is the foundation on which you build the emotional aspect of singing. If you attempt to pour out your soul before mastering the basic technical secrets, you'll probably be asking yourself "Why doesn't my singing sound right?"

The answer is that successful singing requires not only the will and ability to expose your emotions through songs, but also a well-honed technique. Expertise in both areas makes for truly artistic and professional singing. But the emotions are directed *through* the instrument, and the instrument must be fully developed first. Can you imagine playing a piano before all the keys were in place? You'd be limited to whatever sounds the instrument was capable of making at that point in time.

The same is true for singers. The only difference is that rather than going out and buying an instrument, every singer must build his or her voice from scratch. This, however, gives *you* the ultimate control over whether you're playing a cheap, shoddy instrument or a well-crafted one.

The chief aim of *Secrets of Singing* is to give a complete guide to the concepts, techniques and exercises that will give singers of all styles command over their vocal resources.

Ultimately, expression of emotions and your unique experience and personality will surge through the voice into your music when vocal conditions are just right. But this can only happen when you've "built" your voice through technical mastery.

THE IMPORTANCE OF TECHNIQUE

There are basic fundamentals that, in the least, allow any singer to get better and, at the most, allow those with some degree of talent and discipline to turn a seemingly leaden voice into a golden throat.

The magic begins when you've developed a solid mastery of these reliable guidelines. Armed with technique, you'll have the flexibility to make artistic choices and to assert your own unique sound. Your personality and song selections will combine with your technical skill to complete your own "style."

You won't ever have to worry about sounding like a carbon copy of someone else. However, when you're required to sing like (or "cover") another voice, this will be another stylistic option available to you.

Powerful secrets of singing are used by professional vocalists of every style in studios and on concert stages throughout the world. Successful singers eventually discover singing practices that result in confidence. Yes, there are born voices, but there are no born artists. This book reveals the same artistic techniques to you all at once so you can boost your singing capacity at once rather than painstakingly gathering singing technique bit-by-bit through the years.

Real singing know-how is the great equalizer. It's not how much voice you have, but what you can do with your individual vocal resources that matters. A little talent goes a long way with proper training. An immense talent that is also finely trained is certainly one of the wonders of each generation. Artistry is only gained through much perspiration, study and experience.

THE PITFALLS OF "JUST GETTING BY"

Unfortunately, too many singers operate on "survival technique." Survival technique is any mode of singing devised to just get by. The result sounds disappointing and locks the singer into a one-dimensional, colorless delivery. When the objective is to simply get through a piece without cracking or losing your voice, you're not singing; you're merely surviving a performance. Singing in the survival mode is more torture than pleasure, both for the singer and for the audience.

With *Secrets of Singing* and a willingness to practice these techniques, you can learn how to sing correctly the first time and enjoy a lifetime of satisfaction. It can make all the difference.

HOW TO READ
THIS BOOK

"I learned this, at least, by my experiment; that if one advances confidently
in the direction of his dreams, and endeavors to live the life which he has
imagined, he will meet with a success unexpected in the common hours. . ."

Henry David Thoreau
Walden

THE TWO WAYS TO READ SECRETS OF SINGING

This book is written on two different levels for two types of readers. For those who need to sing better *FAST*, there's a huge amount of practical advice that will achieve results *right now*. But it's also a book for singers who want to learn all about the vocal instrument and how the anatomy of the voice affects a singer's performance.

The "Fast Track"

If you need to upgrade your vocal abilities for a recording session, audition, performance, or are having troubles singing your favorite songs or just aren't happy with your vocal quality, read straight through Parts One through Four and you'll find immediate solutions to your vocal problems.

To make it easier to read through *Secrets of Singing* on the fast track, most of the anatomical information and other reference materials are located at the back of the book (in Parts Five and Six). These sections contain very detailed, yet easily readable, information that clearly explains a wide range of vocal subjects, including the physical make-up (in terms of bones and muscles) of the instrument. An understanding of how the voice works is essential for anyone who truly wants to know singing inside and out.

The everyday nuts and bolts of technically polished singing, though, are laid out in Part One. These secrets are so essential and simple that just by reading through them quickly, but thoroughly, many bad habits that work against your natural abilities will be corrected. They allow the mind and voice to work hand-in-hand to accomplish your vocal goals. Singing secrets regarding how to handle the upper voice are laid out in Parts Two and Three.

The truth is that most vocal problems start when the mind acts against your unique talent. That's where the power of these secrets comes in. By getting the mind and the voice working in the same direction, you'll achieve results rapidly.

Getting the Whole Picture

When time permits, or if you prefer to read in depth about the vocal mechanics from the start, refer to the appendices in the back of the book when recommended. By doing this, you'll have the practical know-how to get through any performance situation and the details required to understand the fascinating inner workings of the vocal instrument.

PRACTICE, PRACTICE, PRACTICE . . .

Another important consideration in the presentation of this book is practicing. Schools, private voice teachers and vocal studios everywhere tend to assign singers a lot of vocal exercises and songs to practice.

Although the intentions behind these lessons are good, students often don't know how to practice to achieve the greatest benefit for time spent on their voices. This makes for a frustrating experience for both student and vocal coach.

For this reason, there are several unique chapters which will help you practice effectively, discern what your problems are and locate where in the book you'll find key information. Check the handy Troubleshooting and Question and Answer sections for assistance in quickly identifying specific problems and their solutions.

Powerful practice and performance skills require an understanding of relaxation, posture, and effective practice strategies. Relaxation skills, exercises, and key ideas are described throughout the book (in gray boxes) and special chapters on posture and practicing can be found in Part Five.

Don't Forget to Do the Exercises!

However you choose to read this book, be sure to do the exercises along the way, as specified in the text. There are many types of exercises in *Secrets of Singing*. Some chapters have just one exercise that zeros in on practicing a new concept. There are also three groups of "endurance" exercises in the book. These exercises build the voice, giving it the power and stamina required for the long hours of singing called for during rehearsals and performances.

The exercises that will benefit you most are the ones that don't come naturally at first. With steady practice, however, even these will become simple. These exercises will be your gauge for improvement.

Remember that practice is the only way to train the mind and muscles to react together. When you begin to experience the power behind these simple secrets of singing, you'll be amazed at your newfound level of vocal expertise.

CHAPTER 1

THE BASICS OF BREATHING: LESS IS MORE

"How often does phrasing today sound 'gaspy' because of the intrusion of too many breaths! Let me state unequivocally that when the majority of singers 'need' to take a breath, they really need to RELEASE TENSION, rather than replenish the breath supply."

Weldon Whitlock
Bel Canto for the Twentieth Century

SINGING IS LARGELY IN YOUR MIND. WHAT YOU THINK IS HOW YOU SING!

One of the most common beliefs held by beginning singers is that the voice is completely formed in the throat, at the site of the vocal cords. This is far from the total picture. As you'll see in the following chapters, there are actually many elements that combine to form your "voice."

The foundation of all singing, though, is breathing. Singing requires a strong, controlled breathing system. You'll begin to experience this firsthand by doing the breathing exercises introduced in the "Mastering Breathing" chapter. The voice will begin to relax and show its true potential only after you've begun to master the breath work. Simply understanding how the instrument works, in a step-by-step manner, is the best beginning a singer can make.

MOUTH VS. NOSE BREATHING

Many students ask "Should I breathe through my nose or my mouth?" In the beginning, mouth breathing is preferable because it helps you get a good stretch in the lower breath support muscles and to achieve the feeling of storing the breath low in the lungs. However, both mouth and nose breathing have specific pros and cons.

Breathing through the nose has the distinct advantage of involving the upper passageways where some of the tone will exit (see "Elevating the Voice"). And it can be very helpful in arid climates (like Las Vegas, Nevada) or in places where the air is dry because of air conditioning.

Dry air robs the vocal cords of the natural moisture that lubricates their workings. The nasal passages and sinuses actually humidify air as it passes through them. However, if you choose to breathe through the nose, be aware that a bout with a cold can require a sudden shift to mouth breathing. Also, breathing through the nose can promote shallow (upper chest) breathing.

For most people, it's easier to get a low, filling breath through the mouth. Also, since the mouth is larger than the nose, breaths can be taken in faster with more air inhaled in each breath. For beginning singers or those who've never studied technique before, it's best to start out breathing through the mouth.

In the final analysis, mouth vs. nose breathing is a highly personal matter. Whichever you choose, be sure that each breath is low, quiet, and helps you feel relaxed and ready to sing. Some singers actually successfully breathe through both at the same time. Do whatever feels natural to you.

TAKING THE FIRST STEP

To achieve a strong breathing system, you have to learn how to inhale correctly. Most people consider inhalation (and breathing, in general) an automatic function and something that you don't need to think about. However, in singing quite the opposite is true. A good understanding of how to take a quick, low, quiet breath will provide the foundation for all the following techniques and exercises.

In this chapter, we'll focus on getting air in and out of the instrument efficiently and quietly. While reading the following sections, it's critical that you actually *do* the exercises, not just read about them. Practicing the breathing exercises regularly will improve your singing a hundred-fold. So let's start with the most basic requirement - just learning what a good singing breath feels like.

THE SINGING BREATH

When taking a breath for singing, breathe from the bottom of your lungs up, just like you fill your cup with your favorite beverage in the morning (see Illustration #1.1). When breathing properly, you'll be able to feel the breath *360 degrees around your lower abdomen* (not just in front). The upper chest or shoulders may begin to lift as you're practicing the singing breath. *Don't let this happen!*

ILLUSTRATION #1.1 - Filling Lungs From the Bottom Up

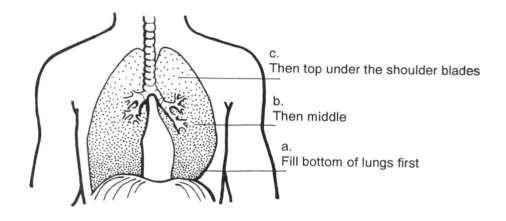

c.
Then top under the shoulder blades

b.
Then middle

a.
Fill bottom of lungs first

To check that you're breathing properly, place the web of your hands in the soft spot between the ribs and the hip bone (see Illustration #1.2). Rest your fingertips on your stomach and your thumbs on the small of your back.

ILLUSTRATION #1.2 - Checking The Singing Breath

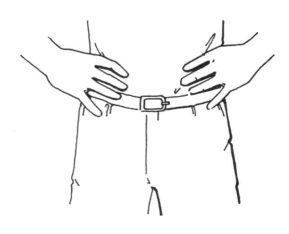

The 360 Degree Secret

One thing's for sure: trying to sing using shallow breathing as your foundation will be an exercise in frustration. Shallow breathing occurs when air is inhaled and stored in the top of your lungs where your neck and upper chest meet. Good breathing begins with the **diaphragm**, and needs additional strength provided by the **breath support muscle group** (see Illustration #1.3). You should literally feel inhalation expanding your front, sides and back simultaneously.

ILLUSTRATION #1.3 - Location of the Breath Support Muscle Group

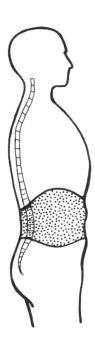

Expansion 360 degrees around your lower abdomen is the key. For most people, this will feel quite different from their normal breathing. Why? Because most of us go through the day taking very shallow breaths. This can be caused by stress or simply allowing lazy living habits to overtake our daily routine.

If you've never studied singing, you're probably wondering: What's the diaphragm and why is it so important? What muscles make up the breath support muscle group and how will they help me to sing better? Turn to Appendix 1 for a full, yet easy to read, explanation of the breathing anatomy. (Or if you need to discover more secrets of singing right away, read on to the next section!)

SIP, DON'T GULP!
(THE QUIET BREATH)

As you're practicing the singing breath, pay special attention to how much noise you make when you inhale. Many singers, thinking that a noisy breath is a deep breath, breathe as if they've just run the fifty-yard dash. In reality, a gasp-like inhalation is one of the primary indications of weak breathing technique.

In singing, silent breathing should be the rule and should be practiced until it becomes second nature. When your breathing technique is strong, inhalation becomes a relaxing moment in singing. Replacing fast, noisy breathing with relaxed, silent breathing inevitably results in vocal poise and technical finesse.

So why do most singers have such a problem achieving a quiet breath? Noisy breathing is usually caused by a constricted throat and is an indication of shallow breathing. Fashion magazines, with their suggestion that the "stomach in, chest out" look is the only acceptable posture, are sometimes responsible for creating habits that cause shallow breathing.

Because of the influence of these magazines, many people worry about looking fat if the stomach protrudes even the slightest bit. Striving too hard for a fashionably flat stomach leads to tension in the abdomen and will sabotage your attempts to take a good singing breath. No matter how hard you gasp for air, you won't be able to get a deep, quiet breath if you're artificially holding in your lower abdomen during inhalation.

NOW, TAKE A DEEP BREATH AND RELAX. . .

It's impossible to overstate the importance of relaxation to the singer. Relaxation is the key to producing one of the fundamental elements of a great voice: The "floating" tone.

When a tone "floats," it seems to defy gravity; it has an otherworldly, ethereal quality. It almost seems to be disconnected from the body. When you achieve this tone quality, your audience will think that you sing as easily and naturally as you breathe.

Without proper relaxation, no amount of practice will give you the "floating tone." More importantly, if you're tense during practice sessions, your body will memorize the sensations of tense singing. Over time this habit will severely limit your voice, and may cause many trouble-filled years down the road.

DON'T SING UNTIL YOU GET RELAXED

No matter what your favorite musical style is, to sing well, you have to properly prepare yourself. Most singers prepare by singing scales, or enthusiastically working through vocal gymnastics known as vocalises. Checking their posture, and making sure that they're breathing correctly may also be involved.

What many singers forget, however, is the most crucial element of great singing: *Relaxation.* It's the key to releasing your unique talent and power. *RELAXATION SHOULD ALWAYS BE YOUR FIRST CONSIDERATION WHEN GETTING READY TO SING.*

LETTING IT ALL HANG OUT

As a singer, tension is your greatest enemy. It undermines the workings of the diaphragm and lower breath support system.

The problem is that most people aren't even aware that they're holding all this tension. After years of "stomach in, chest out" posture, it becomes automatic. To determine if you're carrying tension in the lower abdomen, concentrate on the area between your pubic bone and your bellybutton, as in Photo #1.1a. Don't check for tension too high, as in Photo #1.1b.

PHOTOS #1.1 - Checking for Tension in the Lower Abdomen

a) Correct   b) Incorrect (too high)

Now, just let this area relax, perhaps even letting it become a bit "paunchy," and take a deep breath. If this makes you uncomfortable at first, remember that this work is in pursuit of your dream, *your singing career*. There's no room for simple concerns of vanity.

Now, with your lower abdomen relaxed, sip in the air you would use for singing a phrase of a song. Notice how quietly and deeply the air moves into the lungs. This is what a good singing breath feels like: low, deep and *quiet*.

If you still hear a little gasp-like sound coming from the back of your throat, let a little bit of yawn peel the back of your tongue and the roof of your mouth apart. Literally, set the throat, tongue and mouth in the same position that they'd be in if you were *just beginning* to yawn. The feeling of a slight yawn should be all it takes to make your sips of air completely silent.

STOP, RELAX, AND BREATHE (NOW ! ! !)

Stop right now, before reading any further, and practice at least ten "quiet breaths." Really pay attention to how the quiet singing breath feels. Continue practicing the quiet breath on a daily basis until it's a habit. Don't feel obligated to inhale a large quantity of air when you're practicing silent breathing. It cannot be overemphasized that one of the greatest secrets of singing is that the amount of air it takes to sing is very small.

THE INDISPENSABLE MINIMUM

Not only is the smallest amount of air all it takes to sing, but *less* air gets the job done *better* than more air. It's important to be aware that the vocal cords resist the flow of air at the same intensity at which air hits them from below. So a crucial aspect of singing is that the proper amount of air, which E. Herbert Caesari, in his book "The Voice of the Mind" called **the indispensable minimum**, is delivered to the cords at all times. That is, *in any singing situation, the smallest amount of air that's absolutely necessary to get the job done is the right amount.*

A DELICATE BALANCE

There must be a precise balance between the air pressure from below (moved up by the lower breath support muscles) and the resistance to that air-flow by the diaphragm and the lower ribs. If your support system is too weak, it won't send enough air to the cords, leaving you with a weak, shaky tone. If you're not able to control your breath, too much air may hit the cords, causing them to tighten too much. This is common among singers and leads to a forced sound.

Another consequence of not enough, or too much, air hitting the cords is sharp or flat tones. The cords must vibrate at a certain frequency to produce each pitch. To set this in motion, you need to be able to deliver the correct amount of air to the cords. This will come naturally as you develop an awareness of effective breathing techniques.

THE KEY TO SUCCESS

A good starting point towards developing your diaphragm and abdominal muscles is by doing the breath exercises described in the next chapter. If these muscles are strong and controlled, they'll be able to squeeze a *small* portion of the air out of the lungs, providing plenty of air to sing any phrase.

A small amount of air under pressure from the lower breathing muscles and controlled by the diaphragm and lower ribs goes a long way towards smoothing out and strengthening the voice.

CHAPTER 2
MASTERING BREATHING

"What brings success? Vision, initiative and perseverance. Let the desire to sing command your energies. Let your singing educate and discipline your muscles."

Giovanni Battista Lamperti

GETTING DOWN TO WORK

If you really want to build vocal power, you've got to build breath control *and* support. They go hand-in-hand. They're also exact opposites. **Breath control** refers to how much air you can keep *away* from the cords. More specifically, it refers to how *slowly* the diaphragm and ribs return to their position of rest after inhalation. **Breath support** is created when your lower support muscle group (far away from the cords) powerfully, yet slowly, causes air to be moved *to* the cords.

Consistent practice of the following exercises will strengthen your breathing system and increase your vocal ability tremendously. Reading about how good breathing works must be combined with an awareness of how it *feels* if you want to experience firsthand the benefits of a strong, controlled instrument. It's important that you become familiar with the diaphragm being the major muscle of inhalation. Furthermore, as your breath-work continues you'll sense how the diaphragm opposes or "sits on the air" pressed upward by the muscles of the lower stomach area.

FULL-BODY PREPARATION

Progressive Relaxation

Before working on the breathing exercises, you should relax with exercises that affect the whole body. Start with an exercise that loosens up the body's large muscles. In this exercise, called Progressive Relaxation, you'll drain tension by first tensing, and then relaxing, your muscles alternately from head to toe (see Photos #2.1 A & B). First, lie flat on your back.

Now, bit by bit, slowly begin to tense your entire body, from the bottom up. In the following order, clench your:

1. Toes
2. Calves, thighs and bottom
3. Back
4. Shoulders
5. Arms
6. Hips
7. Chest
8. Neck
9. Face

Squeeze everything as tight as you can and hold for a fairly quick count of ten. Now, just let go and relax completely.

PHOTO #2.1 - Example of
Progressive Relaxation Exercises a & b

a) Tense b) Relaxed

How do you feel? Considerably looser, if you did it right. You've actually squeezed tension out of your muscles the way you wring excess water out of a wet rag.

Try this exercise the next time you feel tense and the desire to practice feels a million miles away. As you squeeze and let go, you'll feel the tension drain away, and relaxation take its place. (You'll probably have a much more positive outlook on your singing too!)

BREATH EXERCISE A: LOCATING THE BREATH SUPPORT MUSCLES: THE PRESSURE RELEASE EXERCISE

This exercise will show you where breath support comes from. Most of us, because of the many sources of stress in our lives, aren't conscious of deep sensations of breath support. You must be able to *feel* this support if you're going to use it for your singing.

HERE'S HOW TO DO IT:

Take a medium-sized comfortable breath through the mouth, again filling the lungs from the bottom up. Feel the stretch in your lower abdomen. Be especially conscious of the lower back and ribs expanding as you inhale while keeping the upper chest calm. Now, begin immediately to exhale. While exhaling, make a "ssss" noise by placing your tongue behind your upper front teeth, just below the roof of your mouth, and squeezing air through a tiny opening between your pursed lips.

Squeeze Out the Last Drop of Air!

Emit the "ssss" sound fairly intensely. When performed correctly, this exercise will sound like a leak in a pressurized steam pipe. Continue making the "ssss" sound as long as you can, being sure to squeeze out the last drop of air. As you're doing this, notice which muscles are working to press the air up to the cords. What you're feeling is the compression of the support muscles around your lower abdomen at work. If you're doing the exercise correctly, you'll feel it in and around belt-level. (See Photo #2.2.)

This sensation is exactly where you want and need to feel support when you're singing. Begin to be aware that breath support should be felt this low (around belt level). In most instances, the support you use for singing will not be as intense as it is in the Pressure Release exercise. However, in certain situations, such as when singing softly or when singing extremely high notes, the sensation of squeezing air may even be this strong.

The general rule of thumb is *if you feel the side walls of your abdomen, or the muscles of your stomach or back <u>rapidly</u> collapsing when singing, you're <u>pushing</u> out air from the lower support muscles rather than <u>pressing</u> out air.* The pressing action used for the Pressure Release exercise is an exaggeration of normal breathing practices. But for those of you who either don't know or aren't sure where breathing ought to occur, it'll give you an immediate feel for the location of breath support.

PHOTO #2.2 - Checking for Proper Location of Pressure Release

Supporting from low in the abdomen protects the cords from strain caused by the air hitting them with too much pressure. This is commonly referred to as *"overblowing"* the cords. When your singing seems harsh and your throat strained, concentrate on *pressing* (rather than pushing) air from deep in the abdomen to the vocal cords.

Daily Practice Works Wonders

Repeat the Pressure Release exercise at least ten times a day. You can practice the exercise as many times as you like until you really feel the movement of the support muscles of the back and ribs and those of your lower abdomen.

WHAT'S SO IMPORTANT ABOUT THE BREATH SUPPORT MUSCLE GROUP?

The considerable strength added to the singing instrument by the breath support muscles gives the feeling that the voice is power-packed. One of the characteristics of great singing depends on your awareness of where support comes from and what it ought to feel like.

If you haven't already read Appendix #1 (and you've got a bit of time on your hands), read it now so that as you're doing the breathing exercises, you'll have a complete understanding of how the breath support muscle group works.

Now that you know how important the diaphragm, ribs, and breath support muscles are, how can you coordinate them to improve your singing? Easy. Just practice the following breath exercise *every day* along with the Pressure Release exercise. Though there are dozens of breath exercises, these two activities produce exceptional results when strengthening and balancing the overall breathing system.

BREATH EXERCISE B: DEVELOPING BREATH CONTROL AND SUPPORT: THE CONTROLLED RELEASE EXERCISE

We all tend to give too much air to the cords rather than letting them take what they need. The following exercise will teach you that it really only takes a little bit of air to sing.

If you send too much air to the cords, they react by closing or tightening too much. When singing with ease, the diaphragm and lower support muscles do their work automatically to prevent this condition. This exercise reveals the proper awareness of breath control working hand-in-hand with breath support.

Consistent practice of the Controlled Release exercise will stretch your lung capacity, make the ribs more elastic, and generally strengthen the breathing system.

Inhalation

Here's how the Controlled Release exercise goes. Begin taking a slow, deep, quiet breath - drawing the air as far down as you can to the bottom of your lungs, aiming for the lower abdomen, lower ribs, and the small of the back. All of these areas should expand simultaneously.

After you feel the expansion in your lower abdomen, inhale a bit faster, allowing the breath to fill the middle of your lungs and finally up under the shoulder blades (see Illustration #1.1).

When you've filled your lungs to their capacity, let the air settle for a split-second. Be sure not to lift your chest or shoulders as the last air fills the top of your lungs.

The feeling of expanding the lower rib muscles and stretching the diaphragm away from the vocal cords (while singing!) is what controls your breath. An awareness that the ribs and diaphragm move down and away from the cords as the lower support muscles are rising up is the foundation of a balanced breath support/control system. It bears repeating: the diaphragm has *two* jobs: it furnishes the power for inhalation and then controls tone support.

When you've really achieved a low filling breath, there's hardly anything left to fill in the upper chest at the end of the inhalation. *(Don't try to take large breaths like this when you're singing songs* - there's not enough time. This is an enlarged breath used strictly in practice to define, identify, and place good breathing sensations.)

By repeating this exercise every day, you'll develop such strong breath control and support habits that eventually a mere sip of air will prepare your voice for any singing situation. When correct breathing habits are in place, a simple sip brings in many times more air, twice as fast, as that of a non-singer.

Exhalation - Releasing the Air

Now it's time to let the air out. But don't just let it rush out. The secret to the Controlled Release exercise is this: you're going to hold back the air by gently pursing your lips together.

When doing this exercise, make sure you don't let the lips or throat become tense - this causes a chain reaction that creates tension near the vocal cords. By holding back the air (as if the sensation of inhalation continues as breath is slowly released) and control develops <u>in the diaphragm and rib muscles.</u> Holding your fingertips in front of your lips, the release of air should be barely noticeable as your ribs brace outwards and the diaphragm held low. Allow the release of air to take thirty to forty full seconds (see Photo #2.3)

PHOTO #2.3 - Checking for Good Controlled Release

HOW LONG SHOULD IT TAKE?

In the beginning, try to release the air at this very slow rate for about thirty to forty-five seconds. Don't be discouraged if you're only able to sustain the air for thirty seconds at first. Your ability to control the air flow will increase as you practice. As you develop more breath control and support, set one minute as the goal for the exhalation part of this exercise.

DO THE CONTROLLED RELEASE EXERCISE WHILE LYING DOWN, SITTING AND STANDING

Practice in sets of ten: Practice three breaths lying down, three sitting, and four standing. When possible, start the breath work lying down because that's when you're at your most relaxed. Then try to match the same qualities of inhalation and exhalation while sitting and standing (see Photos #2.4 a, b, &c).

PHOTO #2.4 (a), (b), (c) - Controlled Release

PHOTO #2.4 (a) - LYING DOWN

PHOTO #2.4 (b) - STANDING

PHOTO #2.4 (c) - SITTING

WHEN TO PRACTICE
THE BREATH EXERCISES

Most of the benefit of the Controlled Release and Pressure Release exercises comes the day after you practice, just like when you work out with weights or do calisthenics. Don't practice the breath work rigorously on the day of a performance; it might rob the diaphragm of vital energy needed for an audition or show. However, it's very beneficial to practice the exercises the day before.

On the actual day of the performance, simply do enough breath work and warm-up scales to stretch out the ribs, back and diaphragm (no longer than twenty or thirty seconds each) and you'll be ready to sing. If you're performing all the time, cut down the length of each repetition to twenty to thirty seconds maximum. You don't need a strenuous breath support or control workout if you're singing on a daily basis.

Sustaining long release times of up to a minute can be used as a maintenance (or voice-building) version of the Controlled Release exercise. Daily Controlled Release work will keep your breathing system toned and strong during periods of vocal inactivity.

Never sustain the release to a point where any discomfort or strain enters into the exercise. You'll notice that as you repeat the exercise, over the long term, your duration of release before any strain enters the process will be longer and longer. This increase reflects the benefits of the exercises and the development of your new breath control and support powers.

MAKING THE BREATH WORK
A PART OF YOUR DAILY ROUTINE

In the early stages of voice building, these breath exercises are an important part of the growth process. The Controlled Release and Pressure Release exercises form the foundation upon which all singing efforts depend. Combining the sensations of pressing from the lower support muscles and resisting the resultant air flow with diaphragm and lower ribs is a crucial step in your quest for vocal power and control. As you become more certain of how and where to breathe, this breath work will become a small part of your routine or be replaced by more advanced drills.

There will, of course, be days when you just won't have time to practice. Don't let that stop you! If you miss a day, take it in stride and go back to work the next day.

Before gaining further command of your breathing muscles, here's another tip on relaxation. Remember to periodically assess your tension level. If, during the course of your practice sessions, you feel tension building up (which can happen when you're trying to master a new technique), *STOP* immediately and relax. The following is a good way to lower your tension level.

SLOW DOWN TO GEAR UP

Deep breathing is great for warming up or for taking a "relaxation break" during practice sessions. It stretches out your respiratory system, clears the lungs of stale air, and oxygenates the entire system. The following exercise does a terrific job at all three:

1)   Lie flat on your back.

2)   Inhale slowly for a count of 10 seconds. Fill from the bottom of your lungs (count 1, 2, 3), up through the sides and the middle ribs (4, 5, 6, 7 - *be especially careful that you don't involve your upper chest*), then way back and up under the shoulder blades (8, 9, 10).

3)   Hold the air for a slow count of ten.

4)   Finally, release the air for another slow count of ten (eventually you'll build up to releasing for twenty seconds).

A slight modification of this exercise will help open up the upper breathing spaces. Simply repeat the exercise outlined above with your arms lifted above your head. Repeat the exercise three or four times.

One of the golden rules of singing is that you never sing when you're tense. This doesn't mean that you shouldn't sing when you have a case of stage fright, but that you should make it a habit to sing or practice only after you've relaxed first.

<u>BEFORE READING ANY FURTHER, PRACTICE THE PRESSURE RELEASE AND THE CONTROLLED RELEASE EXERCISES AT LEAST TEN TIMES EACH!</u>

CHAPTER 3

THE PATHWAY OF SINGING

"The human voice is really the foundation of all music; and whatever the development of the art, whatever the boldest combinations of a composer or the most brilliant execution of a virtuoso, in the end they must always return to the standard set by vocal music."

Richard Wagner

LEARN TO VISUALIZE THE VOCAL PATHWAY

Many singers have an incomplete understanding of what happens to air once it leaves the vocal cords. The pathway that breath follows from the cords to the outside world is extremely important in singing. The breath system carries tone naturally to the resonant bones and cavities in and above the mouth. In addition, incorrect thinking can disturb the normal flow of vibration from its origin in the throat to the resonators above. The more clearly you can visualize this pathway, the better you'll sing.

Up, Behind, and Around...

Most people think that air goes straight from the cords to the mouth. *There's no such pathway!* As the air moves to the top of the windpipe, it presses through the larynx or voice box (and the vocal cords which reside inside the box). Vibrating air comes out of the top of the larynx and must make a slight turn to the rear to avoid being cut off by the base of the tongue. (See Illustration #3.1, or turn to Appendix #2, The Vocal Apparatus, for a detailed discussion of the larynx and vocal cords.)

Once the air clears the base of the tongue, it moves up the throat and then forward through the mouth. Some air goes up higher, over the roof of the mouth, and comes out through the nose. And *vibration* is going to go even higher, reaching all the way to the forehead and out to all parts of the skull.

ILLUSTRATION #3.1 - The Pathway of Air

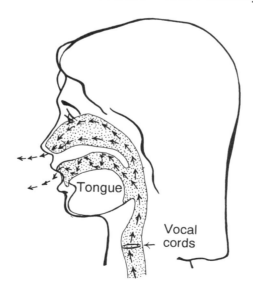

THE PERFECT MODEL:
A BASEBALL PITCH

Study Illustration #3.2 below carefully. The perfect shape to imagine when you're singing is a baseball pitch. Think about what a good baseball pitch looks like: The pitcher's arm swings back, up, and finally forward.

The faster the pitcher intends the pitch to be, the more exaggerated the arch of his arm becomes. He rears back more for spring action and trajectory - to get speed on the ball. Similar motions make up a good tennis serve or golf swing.

ILLUSTRATION #3.2 - Baseball Pitch

THE EXTENDED PATHWAY

The route taken by *vibration* to its release is different than the pathway of air. There is, in fact, no specific place or path vibration takes as it makes its way through the resonators and out of the instrument. Air is directed along specific pathways via the windpipe, tongue, and mouth to the lips and nostrils by virtue of the basic physical make-up of the upper respiratory system. Vibration, on the other hand, once it leaves the cords, goes everywhere all at once, filling the head, mouth, throat and chest with sound (see Illustration #3.3).

ILLUSTRATION #3.3 - Vibration Leaving the Cords

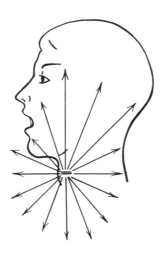

For the purposes of keeping the throat open and maximizing the potential for tonal brilliance or focus, it's very helpful to use certain specific imagery to consolidate the power of your mind as it helps your tone along an extended pathway that mirrors and enlarges that taken by air. Shaping these concepts accurately can help the inner parts of the voice achieve advantageous muscular settings.

To sound rounded and pleasing to the ear, the pathway needs a significant arch. The action is something like a boomerang. You toss the voice back, up and over along the pathway and it returns rounded and enriched to the front parts of the face and head (Illustration #3.4).

ILLUSTRATION #3.4 - Imagery for the Pathway of Vibration

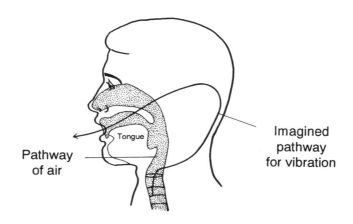

Thus, in the previous illustration, the pathway is gradually extended behind and above the roof of the mouth by degree, depending on how high singing demands the voice to go in terms of pitch.

For low notes, thinking of the route taken by air through the nose and mouth will be sufficient. For higher notes, the pathway continues to lean further back, up and over until it literally follows the outline of the skull itself (Illustration #3.5).

The thought of this great arching pathway opens the throat and allows tone access to the vast network of resonating spaces above the cords. In this way, a full complement of head tones can be added to the voice.

For the uppermost notes of the voice, extend the pathway beyond the bounds of the actual physical outline of your head. After all, the voice is in the mind! In actuality, all this imagery work helps to keep your soft palate lifted and the back of the throat open. If you can imagine a pathway with enough arch, even the highest notes of your voice will come within reach.

ILLUSTRATION #3.5 - Extended Pathway for Upper Extension

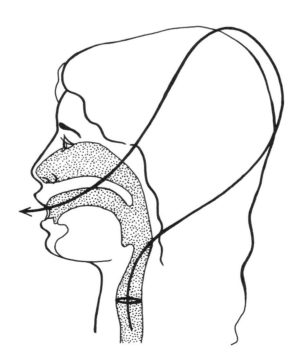

VOCAL PROBLEMS CAUSED BY
INCORRECT VISUALIZATION

The pathway of singing must be memorized or problems will develop. For example, if you conceive of the voice moving directly back, imagining this path will push the air too far back and it'll get caught in the throat (see Illustration #3.6a). This muffles your tone and causes it to lose its rich, ringing sound.

Likewise, if you're visualizing the pathway as a straight line ascending vertically, instead of an arch sweeping back, up, and over the tongue, the vibrating air will be caught and trapped too far forward inside your mouth (see Illustration #3.6b). This causes the tone to be harsh. In order to get a bright, yet rounded tone, air must arch back, up and over the tongue to the highest reaches of your head resonators and imagination.

The pathway is *not* straight back, *not* straight up and it bears repeating that it is certainly not straight forward (see Illustration #3.6c). It is the tongue's position in the mouth which insists that the route air takes to the outside world is slightly back, up and over.

ILLUSTRATION #3.6 (a) (b) (c) - Incorrect Pathways

a) Straight Back   b) Straight Up   c) Straight Forward

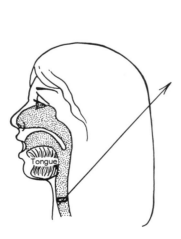
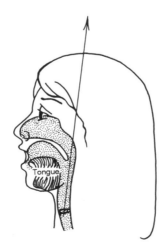
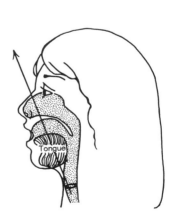

THE VOCAL EXERCISES

The time has come to put these breathing and pathway ideas into vocalized practice. Do you know how the great Michelangelo approached sculpting? He took a raw chunk of marble and chipped away everything that wasn't part of the finished sculpture he saw in his mind's eye.

Michelangelo didn't raise his raw marble into a state of timeless magnificence by just quietly polishing it. No. First he had to remove large sections of stone that didn't fit into his vision of what a piece should look like. Then, he fine-tuned his efforts into a masterpiece. Likewise, achieving the subtleties and nuances of singing comes at the end of your training, not the beginning.

You've got to show equal boldness with your voice. When you practice, work for the fullest tones you can get. Do this above everything else. Those full, strong notes may sound off-key at first. You're going to hit some wrong notes, your voice might even crack. To be perfectly honest, it will take some time before your voice performs the way you want it to.

PERSEVERANCE PAYS OFF

Realize that you're refining the raw materials for your finished instrument. In the study of singing, you have to be willing to make unpleasant sounds at first, in order to achieve the beautiful sounds you know you can make.

Just be sure to bring big, strong sounds to the exercises and songs you sing, and produce them thoughtfully, according to the guidelines presented in these pages. With regular, effective practice habits in place, beautiful, ringing tones essential to great stage and studio performances will characterize your vocal efforts in much less time than expected.

CHOOSE YOUR PRACTICE AREA WISELY

It's a good idea to find a place where you can work without being disturbed. Being able to sing out freely is essential throughout the course of your vocal work. If people will be in earshot of your practice area, it may be necessary to politely advise them that they will be hearing work-in-progress, *not* a finished product.

An average vocal practice session requires that you sing somewhat loudly. This means that you've got to *make your mistakes loudly, too.* If you don't choose your practice area carefully, this can cause a lot of stress.

Unfortunately, far too many parents, neighbors, friends and non-singers, in general, have no clue about the vocalist's training process. They can get painfully sarcastic about the mistakes you make while you work. This, of course, makes practicing painstakingly difficult at times, instead of the thoughtful, uplifting workout it should be.

If this is your case, then don't delay: Find a suitable place to practice *NOW!* You must work in a place where you can feel comfortable really letting yourself go.

Where should you look? Your home is always the first, though sometimes not the best choice, to practice. If that's the case, try college music departments, religious institutions, music stores and rentable rehearsal rooms. Use your imagination. Be creative. Perhaps a family member or friend will let you borrow their place for part of the day.

Don't ignore this secret: *Where* you practice can be as important as *how much* you practice. If you practice consistently, but in a place where you're uncomfortable and constantly holding back, you'll memorize the habit of holding back - the opposite of singing. So before you begin serious practice sessions, be sure you have a practice spot where you're free to sing as loud as you want, *on key or off.* Your success as a singer is at stake.

ABOVE ALL, STICK TO YOUR GUNS!

Non-singers have a very hard time understanding how the raw sounds of practice, with time, are turned into beautiful singing tones. Don't let anyone's comments disturb you. Carry on with your vocal work. You and your vocal coach alone are able to properly evaluate your work.

Everyone who sings in the shower thinks they're a vocal expert. *They're not!* Listening to too many peoples' advice as to how you're progressing is as confusing as seeking out no advice at all.

DON'T CONFUSE PRETTY WITH BEAUTIFUL

Too many inexperienced vocalists make the same fatal mistake when they practice: they try too hard to make **pretty** sounds. Ironically, that's a recipe for failure, not success.

Effective singing doesn't come from making "pretty" sounds. "Pretty" doesn't begin to cover the emotional range you need for professional singing. Strive instead for **beautiful** singing, in which you produce a tone that can carry the full spectrum of your emotions.

It takes *volume* to get big, full tones. In soft, delicate passages, it's risky business to bring your full voice and a rich palette of emotional feelings to the performance.

Sing out when you practice, even at the risk of producing unpleasant sounds. The fullness of tone needed for professional singing isn't achieved by holding back; you achieve it by learning to relax, and then giving out the voice under those relaxed conditions. Practicing and relaxation go hand-in-hand. The right place to practice will help to get you off to a good start. The last thing a singer needs is to add a tense rehearsal situation to the vocal training process.

HOLDING IT IN WILL HOLD YOU BACK

Physical tension has many sources. One is the daily routine, where most of us find ourselves unable to express emotions. A typical scenario: Your boss reads you the riot act. You'd really like to explode, but find yourself trapped between expressing yourself and collecting your next paycheck.

So day after day, emotions are suppressed, instead of let out. Where does all this unreleased energy go? The body has no choice but to transform it into physical energy. There are two options: Work off the energy through exercise and relaxation, or let it accumulate in the muscles.

The body soaks up this excess energy in many places, but, for most people, the shoulders and neck are affected the most. Unfortunately, tension tends to move and gather at the most vulnerable points - usually where it is least desirable. Tennis players get tennis elbows, baseball players get sore shoulders... and singers get frozen diaphragms and rigid, inflexible throats.

PAVING THE PATHWAY WITH RELAXATION

A tense throat blocks air from moving up onto the pathway. The greater the tension in the throat, jaw and shoulders, the more the pathway is cut off. The voice literally has a "thin" sound, because the constricted pathway limits the flow of air.

What's more, with lots of tension in the neck, jaw and shoulders, there often is equal tightness in the inner muscles of the voice box and breathing machinery.

The number one way to relax the voice is to relax your body. Tension arising anywhere else tends to end up in the neck and shoulders. To get rid of this pressure, you first need to become aware of how much tension you carry.

Make it a part of your routine to assess tension many times throughout the day. You can do this when you're waiting in line at the market, while you're driving, etc. When you find yourself nearing the boiling point, take a time-out to relax. Take a few slow, deep breaths. If you're very tense, practice one of your favorite relaxation methods until you've brought your tension down to a comfortable level. By doing this, you'll train your body to maintain a more generally relaxed composure.

STOP!!!

Before practicing the following exercise, take the time to assess your tension level. If you're carrying a lot of tension, take some time to wind down. Above all, *don't sing until you're relaxed!*

USING THE COMPACT DISCS

Included with your purchase of this book are two cassette tapes of vocal exercises. CD #1 contains the medium-low voice version of the exercises and on CD #2 you'll find the high-voice version. It's a good idea to start practicing along with CD #1. This insures that, as you familiarize yourself with the exercises and begin piecing together the technique in your mind, the vocal work will be carried out in a comfortable range. This is not to say that some of the more advanced exercises won't be challenging, but CD #1 is definitely easier than CD #2, and is the appropriate starting place for most singers.

On the other hand, if you're confident that your voice is a soprano or tenor, you may want to start out on CD #2. If it is too difficult, go back to CD #1 and continue practicing until you can comfortably work into the exercises on CD #2.

Similarly, if you know for sure that you're a bona fide bass, baritone, mezzo-soprano, or alto, CD #1 provides the correct set of exercises for you.

If you're unsure what voice type you are, consult with a local choir director at a school, place of worship, or with the person most knowledgeable about voice that you currently know. If you start with CD #1 and it becomes very easy, very fast, you're probably a soprano or tenor. If CD #1 remains challenging and CD #2 is insurmountably frustrating, you're probably a bass, baritone, mezzo-soprano, or alto.

EXERCISE #1: THE FIVE NOTE SCALE: COMBINING LOW BREATHING AND PATHWAY

Now let's put the good breathing habits you've learned together with relaxation and the idea of the pathway. Before singing, take the practice poster that comes with the book and hang it on the wall of your practice area. It has many visual aids that will help you keep the right thoughts and images in mind as you sing through the exercises.

The first vocal exercise looks like this. You will find a sample performed for you at the beginning of the CD.

<Musical Example: The five note scale>

Now, simply sing along with each five note scale, up and then back down. (A scale is a set of notes that are ordered according to pre-set musical rules that determine which notes are to be included.) Use the vowel AH as in the word "father." Use a medium volume and sing each scale starting with a low, quiet breath. Be sure to look at the pathway as depicted on the poster as you sing along with each scale.

Keep each breath low, quiet, and sip-like (no gulps); gently squeeze air up to the cords by using the lower support muscles (as you did in the Pressure Release exercise), and imagine your tones sailing back, up and over the pathway.

Repeat the exercise as many times as you like and practice until you feel that you've got the hang of it - low inhalation, squeezing air up from the low muscles and aiming the air along the pathway.

CHAPTER 4

ELEVATING THE VOICE

"There is a far too prevalent tendency to shirk the real hard (technical) work which must be accomplished before lasting success can be attained. No matter how naturally talented any individual vocalist may be, he or she cannot possibly produce the best results as a singer unless the particular organs have been subjected to a proper and sufficiently long course of training."

Enrico Caruso

Getting the voice up onto the pathway can sometimes be a job in itself. Our moods, health, and relative use or non-use of the voice determine how "in place" the instrument feels. There are some simple ways to gain access to the elevation and movement the voice naturally has when the feeling of singing is right.

THE INNER SMILE

Singing with a smile. It's not a bad idea for many reasons. Not only does a smile light up your face and help an audience enjoy your performance, but it adds natural lift to the voice. The smile (or "sorrisso" as the Italians call it) is a subtle technique that requires careful attention to detail.

Otherwise, at any given concert, you might see singers grinning their way through tragic arias, melancholy ballads and angry rock anthems. Unfortunately, a teacher who asks a student to *grin* while singing didn't care to reveal the fine points of the technique.

The Inner Smile Is An Unseen Smile

You shouldn't be able to see the inner smile. You *feel* it slightly, and in the beginning you may need to exaggerate it a bit. Eventually, though, it must be hidden in the general mouth shape itself. Its presence will help hook the tone up into some of the most effective bones and cavities of the instrument and raise the soft palate (velum), that fleshy portion of the roof of your mouth that lifts when yawning.

PHOTO #4.1 a & b - The Inner Smile

a) Correct   b) Incorrect

Notice that in Photo #4.1a, there's just a little hint of a smile as the singer gives out a tone. This smallish hidden grin is all that's needed to assist the voice in lifting up onto the upper portion of the pathway. When the smile becomes obvious and over-done (as in Illustration #4.1b), tone quality deteriorates and a singer's intentions may be questioned by the audience.

BONE AMPLIFIES TONE

Along with lifting the voice into the head resonators using the inner smile, it helps to think of the bones of the cheeks, eye sockets and forehead as being a huge, bony cavity. Feel as if you're not only lifting the voice, but secretly smiling it up into big, thick bony ridges and caverns.

Seek bone and avoid the fleshy parts of the inner cavities of your head. Bone ampli-fies tone, flesh absorbs vocal vibration. Seek out bone unless you want to dampen your sound to blend as when singing with a chorus. In that case, allowing some of the tone into the fleshy parts of the back of your throat can help to round and darken the voice to "fit in" with the overall choral texture.

For solo singing, however, as when singing a leading role in an opera or musical, or fronting a jazz or rock band, the voice needs to ring out as much as possible. In these cases, lift the voice into the most vibrant bones and cavities available.

GETTING IN THE MOOD TO SING

The sense of a small inner smile is lost when you're not in the mood to sing. *Don't sing if you don't feel like singing.* If you have to practice, perform or record when you're not in the mood, do what you need to do to put the smile back into the tone.

For every individual this process is different. Some people do relaxation exercises (see the gray boxes contained in this book for some tried-and-true relaxation tips). Others try yoga, calisthenics, go for a walk, or take a shower. The point is, *it's essential that you get yourself in the mood to sing.*

If you're not ready to sing emotionally and physically, it's very hard to lift the voice into place. You must bring a bottom-line or "threshold" amount of energy into the singing process just to get the voice off the ground. Otherwise, it will seem no technique can come to the rescue of your vocal efforts. It takes energy to mold the ingredients of technique together. When you gain your composure and feel like singing, the voice will more readily lift up into the cheek bones and head cavities.

THE 90%/10% RULE

How much air should exit through the mouth and how much should go over the roof of the mouth and out through the nose? For most singing situations, the basic rule of thumb is 90% through the <u>mouth</u> and 10% through the <u>nose</u> (see Illustration #4.1).

ILLUSTRATION #4.1 - 90%/10%

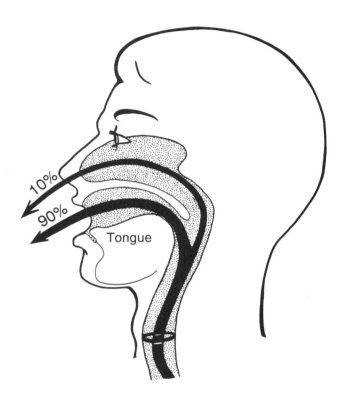

Be Aware! ! !

Many factors can cause the air to fall down and exit too much through the mouth. If you're tired, tense, using a wrong pathway or mouth position, or are not aware that you should be allowing 10% of the air over the roof of the mouth, the voice is not going to go up and over. And consequently, your tone is going to suffer.

Proportion Is the Key

Many singers are afraid of sounding nasal, so they try to make all the air exit through the mouth. However, if you don't permit any air over the roof of the mouth and out through the nose, your tone will sound forced, like you're yelling rather than singing. To get to your unique sound, you need the proper proportion - about 90% of the air exiting though the <u>mouth</u> and 10% exiting through the <u>nose</u>.

USING THE 90%/10% RULE FOR LOW NOTES

The 90%/10% rule is equally important when you're singing in the low part of your voice. You still want the 10% exiting through the nose so your low notes stay connected to the upper resonance. Remember, the key word is proportion, which is exactly what the 90%/10% rule gives.

ROLE REVERSAL: 90%/10% IN THE UPPER EXTENSION

When singing in the extreme top notes of the voice (the upper extension), it can be very helpful to *imagine 90%* of the *air* going out <u>through your nose</u>. This will insure that you get at least the regular 10% of the air going over the roof of the mouth and out through the nasal passages.

Physically, you can't really put a full 90% through the nose when you're singing. But by imagining more air going up the pathway and through your nose, you add lubrication and "ping" to the high notes, making it much easier to sing in the upper extension of your voice. *Remember, never sing "into" the nose, but "through, around, above or behind" the nose.*

Drop Your Jaw!

If you try this technique and the result is nasal, you've imagined 90% of the air moving over the roof of your mouth to the nasal passages, but haven't opened your mouth enough.

If you're really in the upper extension of your voice, any added nasality will be absorbed. *You almost can't be too nasal when you're singing high notes <u>if</u> your mouth is open enough.*

EXERCISE #2: INITIATE A TONE, HOLD FOR FOUR COUNTS

Here's an exercise that allows you to practice the basic operation of getting a tone up in place along the pathway.

<Musical Example of Exercise #2>

On an AH vowel, with good mouth position, lift a tone (with an inner smile or by thinking 90% over the roof of the mouth) and drop it onto the down side of the top part of the pathway. That's what elevating is all about (see Illustration #4.2). Getting each tone you sing to feel as if it starts not at the bottom or middle of the pathway, but is let down on the pathway from high above and behind it is the trick. Hold each tone for four counts.

As you hold the note, be sure that controlled breath, pathway, and inner smile are all included and then stop (or release) the tone gently.

ILLUSTRATION #4.2 - Elevating the Voice

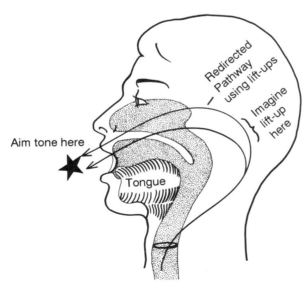

RELAXING THE BACK AND SPINE

To understand why it's important to take the time to loosen up the spine and back, consider this: The spine acts as the main power line for your nervous system. It serves as the primary conductor and switching center for two types of transmissions from the brain:

- Nerve impulse transmissions - these signals from the brain cause muscles to contract or relax. They also coordinate the movements of groups of muscles;

and

- Emotional transmissions - these signals, when used appropriately, energize the voice and bring out your unique emotional interpretation of any song.

For your instrument to perform well and your body to feel well, these transmissions must flow smoothly through your spine. Tension can inhibit this flow greatly.

NO PAIN, NO STRAIN!

A GENERAL WORD OF CAUTION ABOUT STRETCHING EXERCISES: *Use common sense!* Ease slowly into each exercise, going at your own pace. Don't strain or hurt yourself in your efforts to relax.

NOTE: If you have back problems, hypertension, or any other health problem, please consult your doctor before beginning any type of exercise.

In this section, the objective is to relax the spine and back muscles. Here are some effective ways to do just that:

SIMPLE BACK STRETCH:

1) Sit on the floor. Then lean forward and try to touch your toes. Grab whatever part of your legs you can reach (i.e., your calves or ankles) and pull yourself along until you can touch your toes (see Illustration #4.2). Gently lock your knees if you can, without forcing it.

2) Try the same exercise standing up.

3) It's not how far you stretch, but how long you stretch that counts. Try to hold each stretch for at least a minute and a half.

PHOTO #4.2 - Simple Back Stretch

Another great stretch for the back and spine:

1)   Lie flat on your back.

2)   Become aware of the length of your spine; feel the small of your
      back in touch with the ground.

3)   Now pull your knees up, so the whole length of your spine touch-
      es the ground. Try to feel a widening and lengthening of your
      back - up, down and diagonally.

4)   Next, just lie still. Let yourself grow calm, and allow your breath-
      ing to become slow and even, similar to how you breathe when
      you're just drifting off to sleep. Remember to let your breathing
      become *slow and even*. Allow the body to simply exist between
      breaths. Don't even feel like you have to breathe. Let your body
      breathe for you.

CHAPTER 5
FOCUSING THE VOICE

"The biggest single factor in becoming a singer is wish, desire, urge, want, and an all encompassing need to become a singer, no matter what the odds."

Musical Courier

THE END OF THE PATHWAY

Air and vibration, at the end of the arching journey through the head resonators, must be given a final enhancement known as *focus*. Like the proverbial pot at the end of the rainbow, our vocal pathway ends in one of the richest sources of vocal resonance.

Focus assures a comfortable singing tone, that also carries or projects well as it leaves the pathway. Correct focus, or "point" as it is sometimes known, will not only give your voice more ring, but it will smooth out some of the rough edges as well. To understand how to focus your voice effectively, you need to know a little bit about an area of the instrument known as the mask.

THE MASK IS THE TARGET

Directly above, behind, and beside the nose are the nasal resonators. This area consists of small bones surrounding or accompanied by small cavities (see Illustration #5.1).

ILLUSTRATION #5.1 - Bones and Cavities of Nasal Resonators (side view)

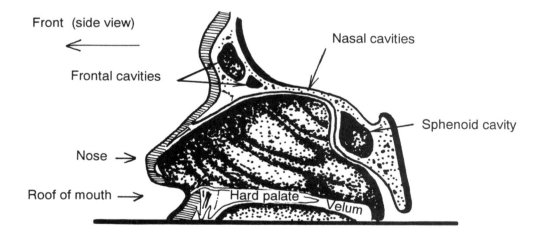

In addition to the nasal resonators, there are resonators located in the cheekbones and the forehead (just beneath and above the eyebrows). Together, these bones and cavities form the powerful resonator known as the **"mask"** (see Photo #5.1 and Illustration #5.2). This is a good time to read "The Resonators" in Appendix 3 to familiarize yourself with the voice's natural amplification system.

THE MASK

PHOTO #5.1   *ILLUSTRATION #5.2*

 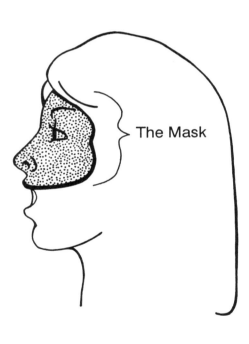

How the Mask Affects Your Tone

When you sing correctly, the mask takes the vibration formed and shaped in the voice box, throat and along the pathway and fine-tunes it, adding brightness and carrying power.

FINDING THE VOICE'S FOCAL POINT (AIMING AIR)

You may be wondering at this point how to achieve focus. As with our use of the mental construct of a pathway, much of this is done by using images that allow us to make adjustments to certain groups of muscles that are normally beyond our will power.

One powerful image is to imagine a wall between you and your audience. Now, visualize a small hole in the wall about the size of a dime (see Illustration #5.3).

In this way, sing through the hole in the imaginary wall. Just thinking of aiming the voice through a small hole in an imaginary wall will affect the muscles of the throat, causing them to consolidate the air into a more pointed configuration.

You aim the air the same as you would aim a dart at a dartboard. Knowing that you want to hit the bullseye, you visualize where the bullseye is and then direct your arm to throw the dart towards it.

Another good way to visualize focus is to think of the difference in concentration between the light of a flashlight and that of a laser beam. When you focus your voice, you're attempting to make it as much like a laser beam of sound as possible.

ILLUSTRATION #5.3 - Aiming the Air

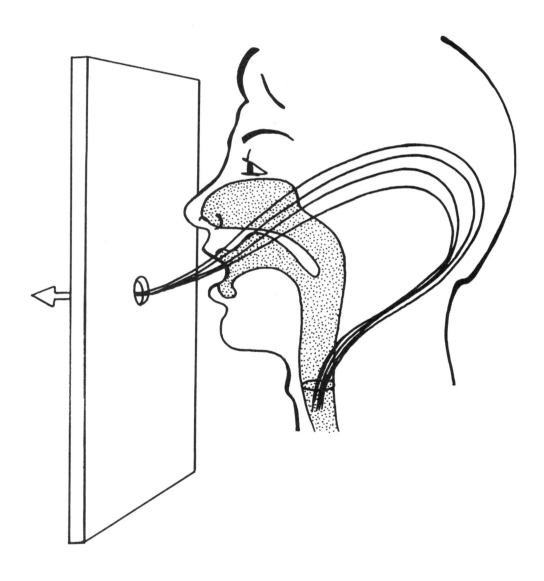

A Word of Caution

The voice must freely and naturally fill the mouth, bones of the head, deep recesses of the throat, and even filter down into the chest all at once. Focusing the voice into or against the bones of the mask and hard palate (by using the image of the hole in the wall) is only one aspect of powerful tone reinforcement. Directing the voice into this forward position <u>only</u> usually leads to forcing, destroying the feel of free resonance and making the pronunciation of certain vowels, such as AH and OO almost impossible.

The mouth, throat and chest must also fill with vibration as well. If you feel the hard palate or teeth reverberate it's a good sign, indicating freedom in the spaces below. But if you try to obtain vibration of the mask by *too* eagerly directing vibration against it, your tone is apt to lose quality and perhaps some of its natural vibrato.

The voice that "pings" or rings in the front bones of the mask should merely be reflecting overall relaxation of the instrument (as well as a throat and mouth that are also full of vibration). When moving freely along a relaxed pathway, the voice is simply magnified in the bones of the mask up front.

THE EARS' "FOCAL POINT"

Most of us evaluate our singing based on what we hear coming back to our ears from the room around us. However, this is an unreliable gauge of performance. Why? Because each of our sensory organs has a specific focal point.

For instance, if you placed a piece of printed paper just a few inches in front of your eyes and tried to read it, you wouldn't be able to, because it's too close to your eyes. But if you put it at a specific focal length, you'll be able to read it easily.

The same is true of the ear. Your ear is too close to your mouth to give an accurate reading of how you sound. This distortion becomes worse as the voice gets higher. For this reason, you must learn to trust the *internal feeling* of good singing, rather than relying on what you hear in the room around you.

HOOKING THE VOICE INTO THE MASK

A singing tone generated at the vocal cords, which fills the mouth and throat, and is then released along the pathway to find its home-away-from-home in the mask, will always seem loud enough to you when singing.

However, if the voice is cut off from these upper resonators, you'll feel it isn't big enough, because you can't hear the natural resonance *inside* your head; you only hear what's happening on the outside.

Avoid Overblowing the Cords!

Unfortunately, when singers feel they aren't projecting well, in a knee-jerk reaction, they tend to force too much air into the throat. This only causes more trouble.

When the tone is properly laid into the mask from the pathway, you won't be tempted to crush the cords with too much air. When focused, the entire instrument is far more relaxed - one of the primary objectives in singing.

LEARNING TO FOCUS WITH YOUR "INNER EARS"

There is an interesting and easy way to develop the internal feeling of good singing, and that is by learning to listen with your "inner ears." Practice a few exercises with one ear plugged some of the time (see Photo #5.2a). After you are fairly comfortable doing this, practice with both ears plugged (see Photo #5.2b). This will force you to sing from the *inside out*, rather than from the outside in.

PHOTO #5.2 - Practicing with One Ear Covered

a) Practicing With One
Ear Covered

b) Practicing With Both
Ears Covered

Try doing the same with some of your favorite songs - you'll probably find this a little unnerving at first. After years of using your outer ears to check your sound, suddenly switching to inner hearing is quite a surprise. While not hearing the outer sound echoing off the walls in the room around you, the inner sound of your voice will at first seem small and insignificant. You will find, however, it contains many helpful hints that can assist in controlling your voice.

Practicing in this manner will cause you to use less air. And more often than not, the less air you use, the better. When you concentrate on what you sound like on the *outside*, you tend to over-sing. By zeroing in on the *inner sound* and the feeling of vibration moving through the pathway to the bones and cavities of the mask you will eliminate one of the causes of over-singing.

THE BENEFITS OF SINGING FROM THE INSIDE OUT

Learning to hear your inner sound has many benefits. Singing over a band through a poor PA system or over an orchestra in halls with poor acoustics will no longer be a problem.

Once you learn what focus feels like, you won't need to hear yourself on the outside. You'll know when you're singing well by how it sounds and feels inside.

Singing in this way also allows you to make adjustments to your sound before tone leaves your instrument. Once the sound is outside, you can't make any changes - it's too late. But if you can feel the voice vibrating inside the mouth or striking the mask, you can make subtle adjustments before the air leaves your mouth. You might drop your jaw a little more to allow for a more extended pathway or adjust the position of your tongue, depending on what you hear and feel *inside*. This is another tremendous advantage of singing from the inside out. (Of course, this system of covering or plugging one or both ears should only be carried out in practice sessions or rehearsals.)

THE FEELING OF GOOD SINGING

The physical satisfaction of good singing cannot be overlooked. This is achieved when you begin to know what good singing feels like on the inside. As you continue to practice singing from the inside out, you'll notice that singing is physically very pleasing.

The action of the singing muscles moving air strongly up to the cords gives you a sense of well-being and control. And the feeling of the cords accepting the right amount of air is an extraordinarily pleasing sensation. Most of all, the sensation of air and vibration arching up through their pathways, filling the mouth and then moving forward to the mask should be an exhilarating and solid feeling. All of these inner elements combine to give you a sense of control, *whether you can hear yourself on the <u>outside</u> or not.*

When first learning to sing correctly, the capacity to feel the mechanical workings of the instrument is foggy at best. The better you sing, the more sensations like focus and pathway become real, not just theories. This awareness is the element that, when added to your singing, allows you to be in control of your voice under any circumstances.

Try a few minutes of *inner* singing every day. After you get used to it, your concentration will be properly divided between your outer and inner sound as well as on the *feel* of the voice moving along the pathway, filling the mouth and focusing in the mask.

<EXERCISES #3(A): TRIAD MELODY>

Listen to the sample on the accompanying exercise CD. Exercise #3(A) looks like this:

<Musical Example of Exercise #3(A): Triad Melody>

Using an AH (as in "father") vowel once again, sing along with each of the following triads (a musical chord where each note is played one-by-one). Your job here is to get each tone to move through the imaginary hole in the wall (see the poster). Take a low breath, support from belt level, and gently, but firmly, blow each tone along the pathway and finally out through the imaginary focal point.

Sing energetically, but try to pace yourself so that you give equal emphasis to each note. Take one small sip between each repetition of the note groups as in the example. And remember, don't clobber the first note of each repetition.

EXERCISE #3(B)

If you're not sure the voice is coming into focus, consider using the word "sung" to get you there. As the tongue moves up to the roof of the mouth to make the "ssss" sound, it literally points out where to focus the voice: the tip of the tongue and behind the top two teeth. Try an exaggerated "ssss" like the one used in the Pressure Release exercise to be sure your lower support system is moving air up onto the pathway. Then, sing the triads on the last two sounds - the "ng" of the word "su<u>ng</u>. It looks something like this on paper:

<Musical Example of Exercise #3(B):
Finding Focus Through A Nasalized Tone>

SSuh - NNNNNNNNNNG

By singing through each passage on NG, the frontal or mask resonators will be warmed and opened. Try for the feeling of NG, vibrating through the whole mask. Avoid humming or, in this case, trapping "NG" in the nose, but rather, lead the vibration through, around or beside the nose.

Don't let the throat lock up while practicing here. Keep the tongue and back portions of the mouth relaxed and free of tension. Listen to the example on the accompanying sound source to check how to do this variation of the Arpeggios Exercise.

As in all singing situations, you should make sure that you're relaxed before you attempt this exercise. If you're a bit tense, try the following relaxation exercise before proceeding.

RELAXING YOUR ARMS AND LEGS

This exercise will instill a feeling of lightness and relaxation in the extremities of your body. It's also good stage-fright insurance, because it helps prevent fidgeting of hands, arms and legs, should you get an attack of nerves in the midst of a performance. Here's how it goes:

1)   Lie flat on your back.

2)   Little by little, gradually lift your whole leg off the ground.

3)   Hold the leg extended in space. Notice the weight. Concentrate on it. Let your leg feel heavier and heavier, until the weight becomes too much to bear. Then let it flop down to the ground.

4)   Do the same thing with the other leg.

5)   Now do the exercise with your arms. First, lift one arm; concentrate on the weight of the arm, then let it fall down to the ground. Repeat with the other arm.

6)   Take a few breaths and concentrate on the feeling of relaxation in your legs and arms.

7)   Now, back to work! Go back to the first leg and complete the exercise: Slowly lift your leg, hold it up, feel the leg becoming heavier and heavier, and then... FLOP!

8)   Now repeat with your other leg and your arms. Keep at it, each extremity in succession, until they all feel heavy and relaxed. How heavy? When you've relaxed sufficiently, your arms and legs will feel so heavy that you feel you couldn't lift them from the ground - not even if your singing career depended on it.

CHAPTER 6
THE FOCUSED MOUTH POSITION

*"Regard your voice as capital in the bank. . . .
Sing on your interest and your voice will last."*

Lauritz Melchior

YOUR MOUTH SHAPE "POINTS" THE AIR

In the previous chapter, you learned how to mentally direct your breath. Focus is also achieved by physically controlling your mouth shape; if your mouth spreads to the sides, as if a hook was pulling on each side of your mouth, the sound will spread, too.

The correct position of the mouth is a nice comfortable oval with the corners drawn in and the jaw down (see Photos and Illustrations #6.1 a & b below). It's also important that you relax your lips; don't purse your lips or push them outward, as tension can accumulate around the mouth and jaw and create problems.

PHOTO #6.1 (a) (b)

a) Correct   b) Incorrect

ILLUSTRATION #6. 1 (a) (b)

a) Correct   b) Incorrect

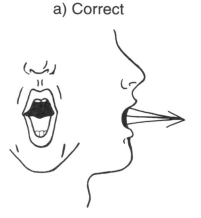   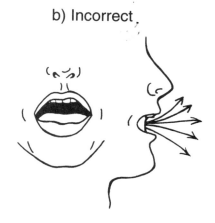

Correct mouth position = focused tone   Incorrect mouth position = no focus

Open Up the Throat With A Yawn

To further open up the area near the base of the tongue, imagine the *beginning* of a yawn. This opens up the pathway, keeps the tongue in the correct position (see Illustration #6.2a) and lifts the soft palate. Keeping some space between the upper and lower molars is always helpful when singing. This done, the back of the throat naturally opens making the critical link between the tone colors of the upper and lower resonances possible.

Moment-to-moment while singing there is an unconscious working of the inner structure of the mouth. Whether on high notes or low notes, the mouth parts continuously move to fine-tune the oral cavity until the feel and sound of any sustained note is just right.

The outer mouth shape is generally opened to the position as shown in Illustration 6.1a. Yet, the tongue, jaw and palate are not rigid, but must be yielding and responsive to the inner directives of the ear. Experience will sensitize you to the feeling of the mouth cavity subtly adjusting to each vowel as it fits into the available space.

Remember, only add the *beginning* of a yawn. If you generate the feeling of a full yawn, the voice box actually becomes lowered too much and creates a new obstruction in the pathway rather than freeing the voice.

Be Aware of Your Tongue Position

Another source of potential trouble in the mouth area is the tongue. Be sure the tongue lies against the back of your bottom front teeth. If your tongue pulls back, you'll cut off the air flow dividing the mouth and throat into two separate resonators (see Illustration #6.2b).

ILLUSTRATION #6.2 (a) (b) (c) - Tongue Positions

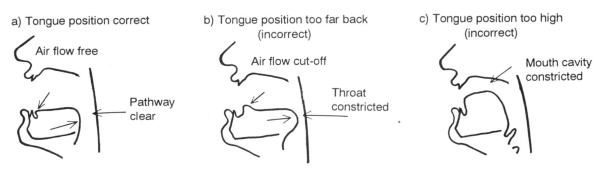

a) Tongue position correct

Air flow free

Pathway clear

b) Tongue position too far back (incorrect)

Air flow cut-off

Throat constricted

c) Tongue position too high (incorrect)

Mouth cavity constricted

The tongue can at times lift too far up. This will lead to the mouth being separated into two separate resonators, front and back (see Illustration #6.2c). This also is not a desirable condition.

The best resonation potential occurs when a flat, forward tongue position allows the whole mouth (oral cavity) and the throat to function as one large resonating space. This is not to say that the tongue doesn't lift, move back and all around the mouth as you form words in general when singing. The optimum oval mouth position, with the tongue flat, its tip touching the back of your bottom teeth, is called for anytime you're sustaining tone on a vowel.

IMAGE: THE REVERSED MEGAPHONE

The focused mouth position, together with the notion of focusing tone (through the hole in the wall) allows for another powerful image to be utilized: that of a *reversed* megaphone, where the small end of the megaphone is up front at the focus point and the big end is achieved by the yawning position of the throat (see Illustration #6.3a). The concept is called reversed not only because the small end of the megaphone is forward at the hole-in-the-wall but also considering that air flow seems to be vacuumed backwards through the mouth to the cords when breath is used firmly yet with suitable restraint.

ILLUSTRATION #6.3 (a) (b) - Reversed Megaphone Image

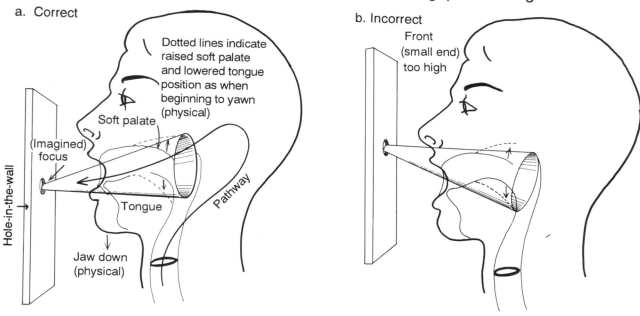

Two of the three parts that make up this image are physically achieved; the other is imaginary. As tone is produced:

1. *Physically,* add the yawn sensation to create the large end of the megaphone that nestles into the back of the throat. Timing is important: add this yawn-like stretch to make the back end of the megaphone (under the soft palate) taller <u>as you inhale</u> just before singing.

2. Drop the jaw. This insures that tone is focused, but allowed to echo in the mouth as a whole. As the voice is mentally focused, the *physical* mouth position must remain open and oval.

3. *Imagine* tone lifting behind and above the megaphone (along the pathway) and then swinging forward, down and out through the reversed megaphone to the hole-in-the-wall.

When singing emotionally charged passages or in the highest range of your voice, simply make the rear of the megaphone taller (add a little more yawn), while keeping mental focus laser-like in size. Remember, the small end up front is *mental* only. *Physically,* the jaw is down and the mouth is quite open to let out the sound. The mentally focused tone will not sound pinched as long as you gently heighten the back of the throat and open up your mouth comfortably.

Also, be sure that the front (small end) of the reversed megaphone doesn't lift up as emotional intensity or volume is added (see Illustration #6.3b). The secret of using this image is to keep the cone-like shape aimed at the hole-in-the-wall *no matter how high in range or how powerfully you sing.*

After working with the reversed megaphone image for some time and when breath support and control are well balanced, you may notice a sensation often talked about by singers; it feels as if air is being drawn *backwards not forwards* (through the hole-in-the-wall and back end of the megaphone) all the way to the bottom of the throat while singing! This feeling of drinking the air while singing only becomes tangible when one consistently uses the smallest amount of air absolutely necessary to achieve the vocal results desired.

MAINTAINING A CLEAR PATHWAY

The bottom line regarding mouth position is to keep a clear pathway when singing. Not only will this eliminate many vocal mishaps, but it will assist in discovering your fullest tone.

Be Gentle With the Jaw

Singing will be difficult whenever the jaw is dropped rigidly, when it is drawn backwards too forcibly, or when the chin juts forward with undue effort. When you sing, the mouth should move towards an oval shape with the corners drawn in and the jaw *gently* let down (see Photo #6.2). The tongue should be lying against the back of your bottom front teeth.

There shouldn't be any rigidity where the jaw attaches to the skull (tempomandibular joint). For more details on jaw and head position, check the Posture chapter in Part 5.

PHOTO #6.2 - Correct Position of the Jaw

EXERCISE #4(A) - ARPEGGIO

In this exercise, we'll take the same triad used in Exercise #3 and put an extra note on top. This turns the group of notes into what's known as an arpeggio (from Italian, meaning literally "harp-like"). Sing the four notes in quick succession and then sing back down again.

<Musical Example: Arpeggio Exercise>

As in Exercise #3, you should sing on an AH vowel. Remember to use the lower support muscles to press air back up and over the pathway and then aim the notes through the reversed megaphone to the imaginary hole in the wall. It's important to pace yourself. Don't blow too much air into any one note.

Be sure to open your mouth to a full oval position *before* the first note and, here's the important thing, *keep the same low jaw position all the way through the ascending and descending parts of the exercise.* This assures tone doesn't sound constricted as you mentally achieve the front end of the megaphone.

If you feel your focus is drifting, preface each note on the arpeggio with an "N" (for example, nah). This is a temporary crutch, so as soon as your focus is improved and the mask feels full of vibration, go back to the pure vowels only.

Use a mirror to be sure your shoulders stay down, your jaw stays comfortably down and that your tongue always touches the back of your bottom teeth (see Photo #6.3).

PHOTO #6.3 - Practicing With Mirror

a) Singer

b) Instrumentalist

EXERCISE #4(B)

You might also try limbering up the jaw by singing the vowels EE and AH over and over again in quick succession. It's a little like the "ee-ah" of a donkey, or chewing with your mouth wide open. Sing along with the arpeggio exercise, as indicated in the sample on the accompanying CD. To add a little focus to this exercise, add an N or M before the arpeggio to help guide the voice through the (imaginary) hole-in-the- wall.

<Musical Example>

Exercise 4

♩ = 160

Version 2: ee - AH - ee - AH - ee - AH - ee

etc.

RELAXING THE TONGUE

The tongue has tremendous potential for capturing and storing tension. And relaxing various parts of the tongue is an important, though often overlooked, procedure to prepare for singing.

Here is an exercise to relax the tongue:

- With a bit of self-massage, work underneath the jaw where you can feel the root of your tongue (see Photo #6.4).

PHOTO #6.4 - Massaging Base of Tongue

RELAXING THE NECK AND JAW

The neck and throat can contain a reservoir of tension that adds rigidity to the jaw. So it's crucial that you learn how to relax this area or it can become a serious bottleneck for the air that flows through your instrument.

A simple but very effective exercise to prepare the neck area for singing is called the neck roll. Simply let the head slowly and heavily roll around in a complete circle (see Photos #6.5 a, b, c, & d).

You might hear snaps, crackles and pops as you go. Don't be alarmed. That's just your body telling you that you need this exercise. In fact, the more snaps, crackles and pops you hear, the more tension you're carrying in your neck, and the more practice you need.

PHOTO #6.5 - Demonstration of Head Rolls - (a) (b) (c) (d)

a)   b)   c)   d)

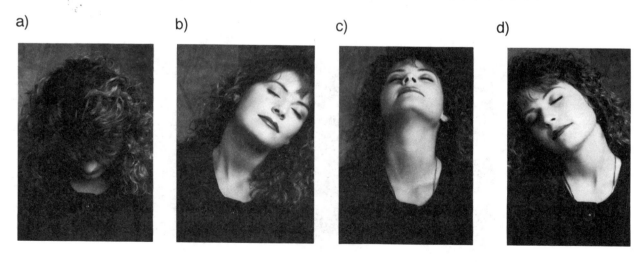

After head rolls, you're ready to try some head nods:

1. Let your head nod to one side, and feel the stretch. Then nod to the opposite side.

2. Next, nod forward and hold it there. Feel the weight of your head. Keep feeling the weight until your head sinks through the tension and eases into a final, comfortable resting position.

3. Repeat to the left, right, and back. Do this exercise slowly and deliberately. Repeat until your neck is completely relaxed.

It's also extremely beneficial to massage the large muscles in the neck, called the sternocleidomastoid (SCM) muscles (see Illustration #6.4). To locate these muscles, turn your head as far as you can to the side. On each side, you'll feel a muscle that extends from your shoulder to the base of your skull.

ILLUSTRATION #6.4 and PHOTO #6.6 -
Locating and Massaging SCM Muscle

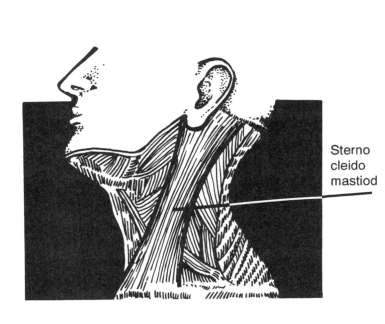

Sterno
cleido
mastiod

After you've found the SCM muscles, again turn your head to the side, and using your fingers, rub across the muscles. Use as much (or as little) pressure as is comfortable for you. When you're able to soften and relax the SCM muscles, the jaw releases, and frees up the whole area around the jaw, mouth, and neck (see Photo #6.6).

Try to do some self-massage *every* day. Spend extra time when you'll be performing or recording, but don't make the mistake of waiting for a big event to practice these relaxation exercises. *The benefits of these exercises accumulate the more you do them, so start now!*

CHAPTER 7

ANCHORING TONE

"To be nobody but myself - in a world which is doing its best, night and day, to make you everybody else - means to fight the hardest battle which any human being can fight, and never stop fighting."

e. e. cummings

ACHIEVING A BALANCED TONE

The feeling of a well-balanced voice is worth the effort and study it takes to achieve such a tone. As William Vennard so aptly states in his book *Singing, The Mechanism and Technique*, the voice always needs "brilliance and depth" *simultaneously*. **"Brilliance,"** comes from the upper resonators in the mask via mentally lifting and focusing tone while physically "fixing" mouth shape to allow for the maximum physical consolidation of tone. **"Depth,"** comes from the lower resonators in the throat and upper chest and must be simultaneously added to the brilliance to insure vocal balance is maintained. Hereafter, lower resonance will be designated as throat/chest resonance to emphasize this intimate connection between these two areas of tone enhancement.

The voice really has three major zones of resonance: the head, mouth, and throat/chest. To achieve a balanced tone, you must balance or equalize these resonances proportionately.

How do you equalize the resonances? The key secret to this balance is to realize the mouth, lying right smack in between the head and throat/chest resonators, is the perfect "mixer" for tone. By keeping it as full of tone as possible, at all times when singing, it combines the two qualities and **anchors** or centers tone (see Illustration #7.1 below).

ILLUSTRATION #7.1 - Where to Anchor and Double-Anchor Tone

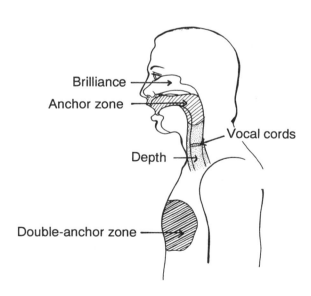

WHAT'S ACTUALLY HAPPENING WHEN YOU ANCHOR TONE?

Tone becomes anchored when the *mouth* simultaneously fills with focused tone from the mask above and resonance from the depths of the throat/chest resonators, below.

As far as singers are concerned, the mouth includes all the inner spaces made available when gently yawning, all the way down to the bottom of the throat. When you seek the sensation of vocal tone "filling the mouth" your search for resonant space should take advantage of the front, rear and lower parts of the mouth cavity.

THE DOUBLE-ANCHORED TONE

When tone is anchored, you'll have the sensation that your mouth is full of whatever vowel sound you're singing. It'll almost feel as if you could chew the vowel sound.

In the upper range, an important image and sensation to strive for is the voice leaning (or vibrating) right on your sternum and chest in general. A double-anchored effect results when the brilliance of high notes is first rounded and mixed with deeper tone colors in the mouth and then stabilized by resting or rooting in the depths of the chest itself. To double-anchor a top note one imagines the support muscles pressing breath right onto the inside wall of the chest before it leap-frogs up the pathway and out through the reversed megaphone. Tone seems to spring from the mask, mouth and chest simultaneously when double-anchored (see Illustration #7.1 and #11.2).

KEEP THE PATHWAY OPEN

With this duality in mind, it's important to insure that the throat, neck and shoulders form a relaxed pathway for vibration. Without a clear path through these areas, brilliance and depth can't merge in the mouth and the voice becomes disconnected and difficult to handle.

When the conditions for combining brilliance and depth are just right, it feels like the lower breath support muscles are pressing tone along the pathway and right into the mouth simultaneously. The small eddy of air that swirls or echoes in the mouth adds roundness to the overall tone.

The mighty combination of upper focus and lower throat/chest resonance, both anchored in the mouth, is an unbeatable combination for stabilizing the voice and relaxing the throat muscles. The goal is to feel *nothing* at the vocal cords, while the resonators are full of vibration.

In fact, under optimum conditions, it seems like the mouth is so filled with vibration that when you open it, the vibrating tone virtually overflows out to the admiring audience. And that's how simple singing should become. You open up the mouth and let out the vibration gathering in the mouth from the resonators above and below.

EXERCISE #5: OCTAVE JUMP, HOLD THREE COUNTS, AND DOWN A SCALE

The fifth vocal exercise is designed to give you an opportunity to work with pulling the "anchored" sensation together. The exercise for this work looks like this:

<Musical Example of Exercise #5>

With your mouth in a good oval position, sing the tones as demonstrated on the CD. Use a comfortable AH vowel, check your breathing and mouth position (see photo #7.1). Be sure to keep your breath sip-like and silent and kick in a good measure of breath control.

PHOTO #7.1 - Checking Breath and Mouth Position

You'll see there is a low sustained note before jumping to the top note and then a scale down. While holding the preparatory low note, fill the mouth with as much tone as possible.

After moving up from the starting note, along the pathway, to the octave note (octave is a musical term for a note of the same name, but thirteen keys higher on the piano), hold and deepen the top tone for three counts and then sing down the scale. See if you can sense your mouth as "full" of vowel on this top note as it was on the bottom note.

While holding the top note for three counts, focus through the hole-in-the-wall and balance the voice in the mouth, allowing in deeper qualities of throat and chest resonance (double-anchor). With focus from above and throat/chest accents from below filling your mouth simultaneously, you'll feel the stability achieved through anchoring tone.

CHAPTER 8

THE FIVE BASIC VOWELS

"The vowel exists first in the singer's ear; if it does not, nothing in the world will enable him to produce it; all the shaping of resonators and learned talk about frequencies are helpless to achieve what the human ear can do, if left alone."

Percy Judd
Vocal Technique

START WITH THE BASICS

In painting, serious artists first learn the rules governing the three primary colors: yellow, blue and red. Only after mastering these colors can they move on to tackle the secondary colors, such as orange, green and purple. After a great deal of work with these basics, the painter is finally ready to combine these colors into even subtler shades which create the emotional moods captured on canvas.

FIVE BASIC VOWELS

Singers also have to start somewhere in mastering the infinite palate of vowel colors. For this purpose, the exercises in this book use five vowels of the English Language: A, E, I, O, and U. A vowel is any sound which originates at the cords in the voice box and passes unhindered through the pathway.

"BASIC" VS. COMPOUND VOWELS

"Basic" vowels are sung as single, rather than *compound* sounds. Take the vowel "i" as in the word "time" for instance. "I" is really a double or "compound" vowel because you have to say AH + ee in rapid succession to produce the entire vowel. Compound vowels are called *diphthongs* (literally "two sounds").

So when singing exercises, let's use the single versions of the five basic vowels, which are EE, EH, OO, OH (OH will be discussed in detail below), and AH. It's essential to begin with the basic vowels because most compound vowels [such as "A" (EH + ee) or "I" (AH + ee)] have a *constrictive vowel* at the end. (Compound vowels will be discussed in detail in Part 4.)

The constrictive vowels, EE and OO, cause the mouth or throat to close, the opposite of what's needed to sing freely. There's no problem with EE and OO when sung individually. Ease of tone production can be gained even with them. But, whenever possible, detach them from compound vowels to allow for more openness in general. Remember, the more open and relaxed your throat is, the better.

Splitting Compound Vowels

A = EH + ee

I = AH + ee

O = UH + oo

TO MAKE SURE YOU'RE GETTING IT RIGHT, USE A MIRROR

As before, use a mirror to check your mouth position as you practice the basic vowels. You might even keep a small pocket mirror with your singing related materials so you can check the shape of your mouth and position of your tongue whenever you practice.

THE AH VOWEL

For most people, AH (as in f<u>a</u>ther) is the most natural of all the vowel sounds. When you make a sighing sound while you yawn, it usually sounds like "Awwwwww…" That's the perfect rounded AH!

Again, when singing AH, just remember the essentials of good mouth position. Drop the jaw, fill the mouth with vowel, and lift the vibration along the pathway into the mask. As you ascend up a scale or sing a high note on AH, add a trace of AW (as in "saw"). The thought of adding a little "w" to the sound helps keep the throat and mouth rounded and open (see Photo #8.1)

PHOTO #8.1 - A Well-Shaped AH Vowel

THE EE VOWEL

This vowel sounds like the "EE" in "meet" and takes a bit of know-how to adjust into a comfortable position. There is a universal tendency to spread the lips into a wide smile-like position when singing EE. When you allow the mouth to spread, the sound becomes shrill and lacks resonance (see Photo #8.2)

The best way to avoid this is to *gently* purse the lips into an OO-like position while singing EE. This position focuses the vowel without changing the unique quality of EE. When you sing higher tones on EE, drop the jaw, add a little extra air, and be sure the tip of your tongue touches the back of your bottom front teeth.

Try to keep the spaciousness of the AH vowel in mind when singing EE. Memorize the "feel" of the space between the tongue and roof of the mouth (in the back of the throat) while singing AH. Try to achieve the same "roomy" feeling on the EE vowel.

PHOTO #8.2 - A Well-Shaped EE Vowel

THE EH VOWEL

The EH vowel sounds like the "E" in "bet" and is fairly simple to produce correctly. Let your jaw fall down in a yawn-like fashion as much as possible. At the same time, touch the tip of your tongue to the back of your lower front teeth and add a slight yawn-like sensation at the back of your throat. That's all there is to it!

Be careful not to confuse EH with the diphthong AY, which is actually EH + ee. Remember, EH is a basic sound that can be sung with an open throat. As with EE, be sure your mouth shape stays oval and doesn't spread to the sides. *You'll note that as opposed to the EE vowel, which is somewhat constrictive, EH allows for a full drop of the jaw* (see Photo #8.3).

PHOTO #8.3 - A Well-Shaped EH Vowel

THE OO VOWEL

OO, as in the word "moon," is shaped much like OH but the opening of the lips is somewhat smaller. The key to successfully handling OO is to be sure the lips remain in an oval, rather than a round, position. Oval lips indicate the jaw is somewhat lowered, which is required even on OO. As mouth space is also somewhat cramped on OO, match the inner feel to that of the AH vowel here too (see Photo #8.4).

PHOTO #8.4 - A Well-Shaped OO Vowel

THE OH VOWEL

Unless sung properly, the OH vowel (as in "boat") is a compound vowel. OH should be sung somewhat "dry" like the "O" in the word p**o**lice. OH is actually a diphthong (UH + oo) whose basic version UH sounds like the "O" in "love" (thus the pronunciation of O in p**o**lice should rhyme with the O in love). To sing OH comfortably, just use the regular rules for good mouth position: drop your jaw, keep your lips oval, launch tone back and up through the pathway and anchor the tone with the jaw down, tongue down, and breath focused through the hole in the wall (see Photo #8.5).

To be sure your UH sounds like an OH when sung, finish off the O with just a hint of OO at the last possible moment. In the upcoming exercises, as you ascend up a scale or sing a high note, allow the lips to shape towards a full-blown oval. *Elongated oval* lips will help keep OH from sounding too yell-like (or becoming a compound vowel).

PHOTO #8.5 - A Well-Shaped OH Vowel

EXERCISE #6 - SLOW SUSTAINED VOWELS

Try singing all of the five basic vowels in succession. It's a good idea to refer back to these pages or the practice poster that accompanies this book as you're doing the exercises to make sure that you keep these and the other secrets of singing in mind. Use a mirror when possible to check that your mouth shape resembles the photo examples for each vowel. Remember, *vowels are the medium through which all tone and expression of your feelings will reach the audience.* To achieve a more complete feel for these vowels, use the next Exercise Group to perfect their shapes and sounds.

CHAPTER 9

THE INITIATION OF TONE

"A tone must be self-starting, self-prolonging and self-stopping."

Giovanni Battista Lamperti

AMATEURS ATTACK; PROFESSIONALS <u>INITIATE</u> TONE

Before singing the first set of endurance exercises, it's important to touch on how to start a tone. This will prevent you from falling into one of the most common traps for amateur vocalists.

To begin a tone, the vocal cords must come together to resist the passage of air. However, the cords must never actually close completely or bang together. *There must be a cushion of air between the cords at all times.*

Often the "attack" of amateurs is due to overly enthusiastic pushing rather than diaphragm-rib controlled gentle pressing of the air into the cords. This habit not only causes an unpleasant jolt at the beginning of the tone, but may be harmful to the cords over the long term.

TIMING IS EVERYTHING

Often the difference between "attacking" a tone and **initiating** one is timing. The movement of the vocal cords must be perfectly coordinated with the pressing of air up from the abdomen. If the air arrives a split-second too early or too late, you'll have a feeling of "missing" the note rather than initiating smoothly.

If the vocal cords and breathing muscles are out of sync, your voice will feel generally weak and ineffective. A lack of precise timing between the cords and breathing muscles is also responsible for many of the problems experienced when leaping to a high note.

THE SECRETS OF SMOOTH INITIATION

Because it takes a split-second for the air pressed from below to reach the cords, you need to *move your breath support muscles before you move your mouth*.

ADD A SLIGHT "H" BEFORE VOWELS

Adding a slight or half "H" before vowels in exercises (or before words which begin with vowels in songs) will help the air get to the cords on time. This little sigh is merely a way to get the air to the cords on time. *It shouldn't be audible when performing.*

If someone listening to you can hear the "H," you're over-exaggerating the sound. Practice this technique in the songs you're working on and in the following exercise.

EXERCISE: SOFTENING INITIATION WITH "H"

To practice softening your initiation, use a song that you're familiar with and concentrate solely on the initial sound of each word, adding a slight "H" to all words *beginning with a vowel*. Here's a segment of Bryan Adams' "(Everything I Do) I Do It For You" (© 1991 Almo Music, Badams Music, Zomba Publishing & Zachary Creek Music Inc.)with all of the half H's marked.

*< **Musical Example #1** > -* Adding "H" to Soften Initiation

(EVERYTHING I DO) I DO IT FOR YOU

Lyrics and Music by
BRYAN ADAMS, R.J. LANGE
and M. KAMEN

(Everything I Do) I Do It for You - 5 - 1

(Everything I Do) I Do It for You - 5 - 2

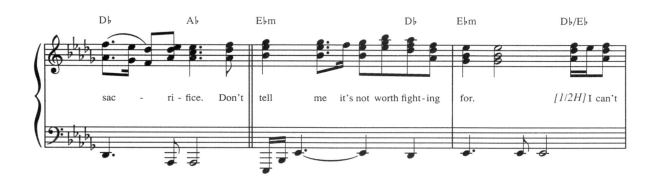

sac - ri - fice. Don't tell me it's not worth fight-ing for. *[1/2H]* I can't

help it, there's noth-ing I want more. You know it's true,___ *[1/2H]* ev-ery-thing I___

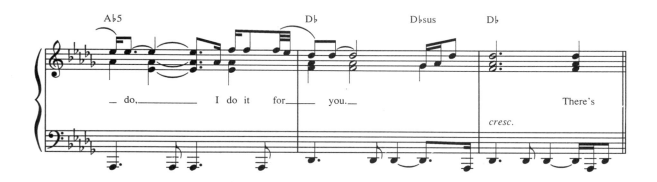

___ do,___ I do it for___ you.___ There's

no love___ like your love,___ *[1/2H]* and no___ oth - er could give

(Everything I Do) I Do It for You - 5 - 3

(Everything I Do) I Do It for You - 5 - 4

(Everything I Do) I Do It for You - 5 - 5

It helps to use a tape recorder to make sure you're not exaggerating too much. Remember, *the goal is to initiate each tone perfectly*, not to add a big, artificial "H" sound. Keep practicing with a tape recorder until you develop a feel for smooth initiation of tone.

Exercise Group 1 will give you a good opportunity to soften the initiation of tone with the "hidden H" sound.

CHAPTER 10

VOCAL EXERCISES:
ENDURANCE GROUP 1

"Whether he is taking a lesson, or studying by himself, the student should retire within a mental circle of song that severely excludes the usual annoyances of life and that petty feverishness which we... associate with civilization."

E. Herbert Caesari

Singing is the ultimate do-it-yourself activity. No one can do it for you, and no one can make you feel good about the discouraging days. No one will get you back to work on it tomorrow. Singing is your job. It's a test of will. But if you find that will, you'll also find the voice of your dreams.

WORKING FOR ENDURANCE

You've performed exercises to help you initiate and anchor tone, and to make your voice sound more appealing. But to meet the rigorous demands of a professional performing career, you'll need yet another kind of training. In order to sing for long periods in concert without tiring, you'll need to develop a voice with consistent power.

The following group of exercises, known as *vocalises,* will help you in that area. They're specially designed to build flexibility, power and endurance into your voice. Of course, they will also help you further refine your technique.

After you master this group of vocalises, there will be two more sets of endurance exercises upcoming in following chapters.

"AH" - THE GUIDE VOWEL

As with the previous vocal work, begin each of these exercises with the AH vowel. Work through the entire group, producing a pure, relaxed AH. Then try to find the same open sound on the other four basic vowels. Especially on EE and OO, try to find the same spacious feel in the mouth/throat as you do on AH.

Sing each set of scales with an easy, medium volume. Don't blast your way through these vocalises - that does more harm than good.

Continue to use a hand-held mirror, so you can check your mouth position, and be sure it stays oval. You also want to be certain your jaw and shoulders remain down throughout the exercises. Do this religiously, until they stay down without any conscious effort.

You might want to check your breathing as well. Here's an easy way to do it: Hitch a belt around your lower breathing muscles. Pull the belt tight, but don't buckle it. The belt should stretch as you breathe; try to feel your ribs, back, and tummy pressing out on it <u>while singing</u>. (see Illustration/Photo #10.1). If the belt doesn't stretch as you breathe in, it means that you're storing your air too high.

PHOTO #10.1 (with overlay) - Practicing With a Belt

Before you sing each exercise with the CD, listen to the examples. While you do so, keep the pathway in mind (look at the poster-sized practice chart, if you need a review). Alternate your concentration between that and the other four vocal principles: checking breath, the balance between pathway and focus, mouth position, and feeling for the anchored tone.

CAUTION!!!

Any voice can be overworked or misused. Once you've passed a certain point of vocal fatigue, you're doing more harm than good. If it feels like you're wearing down your voice, rather than building up your strength, stop and rest the voice.

It's important to include periods of vocal rest along with your exercising. For instance, if you sing for twenty minutes, stop and rest the instrument for five to ten minutes to let the cords and yourself resuscitate.

If at any point you feel you're hurting yourself, stop immediately. If there's any question that you might have strained your instrument, see an ear, nose and throat specialist or your family doctor.

Most normal discomfort due to oversinging will go away within the hour or sometimes by the next morning. If mild pain is disturbing you longer than this, have it checked out as soon as possible. If any exercise on the accompanying CDs is consistently too high for you, leave it out temporarily and come back to it when you've mastered more technique or try the same exercise on CD #1. Good luck and don't forget, where there's a will, there's a way!

A SINGER'S GUIDE TO SAFE SINGING

You may be wondering if singing too much or too hard can damage the voice. If you have this fear, and you overprotect your voice because of it, you need to adjust your thinking.

Look at it this way. Suppose you go swimming on a hot summer's day. You feel so invigorated, you swim lap after lap, and exert yourself a lot more than you had intended.

What consequences would you suffer? You'd probably wake up with sore muscles the next day, especially if you hadn't exercised in a while.

Does this mean you've pushed yourself a little too hard? Yes. But it doesn't mean that the swimming was bad for you! It just means that your body wasn't used to the activity. If you swam just as hard on a regular basis, you'd soon get into shape. Your muscles would grow firm and trim; they'd stop feeling sore the next day.

It works the same way with the voice: when you start to sing with real power, your voice may experience some discomfort at first. But as your vocal muscles get stronger, you'll be able to sing at full intensity without getting tired.

THERE <u>ARE</u> SERIOUS VOICE CONDITIONS

After you've established a regular practice routine, a sudden or unaccustomed persistent throbbing (or any other discomfort around the cords) should be taken seriously. Talk to a voice teacher or see a specialist. Don't ignore it. The same thing goes for a chronic rasp or hoarseness that seems to linger on and on. In most cases, you'll be told it's a case of vocal fatigue. After a few days of rest, you'll be good as new. But never ignore such symptoms.

On the other hand, don't worry about an occasional mild soreness you might feel after a lengthy vocal work-out. When technique is not fully developed, certain improperly sung tones take a toll on the throat. This might be felt as a bit of general soreness in the region of the cords.

Don't fear a damaged voice. Fear an underdeveloped technique.

EXERCISE #7: THE DIAPHRAGM EXERCISE: ASCENDING STACCATO THIRDS

This exercise serves as a wake-up call to the diaphragm. As a matter of fact, it stimulates the whole general breathing system. So, on top of building your vocal endurance, it works as a terrific "quick start" for the voice.

As you sing along with the accompanying CDs, you'll also be strengthening the small muscles of the vocal cords. This gives the vocal bands the power to resist (or bite into) the pressurized stream of air that the breath support system moves through them.

Therefore, with this exercise, you practice a valuable technique: How to balance the power of the breath support system with the strength of the vocal cords as they resist the passing air.

<Musical Example of the Diaphragm Exercise>

(H)AH (H)AH (H)AH, *etc.*

Be sure to keep the tones separated and use a half "H" for each tone to prevent bumping the cords together or singing dry, without air. When done correctly, this exercise will make your tummy jump around just like it does when you're laughing. This happens because your diaphragm moves the viscera out of the way as it springs to action.

EXERCISE #8: DOUBLE 5-NOTE SCALES

This exercise provides you with several pairs of scales. Hum each of those scales. Be sure to hum in a relaxed manner - with the feeling of a "bit of a" yawn in your throat. If your throat feels a little closed, try imagining a small ball, about the size of a ping pong ball resting on your tongue toward the rear of your mouth (see Illustration #10.2).

ILLUSTRATION #10.2 - Imagery of Ball Resting on Tongue

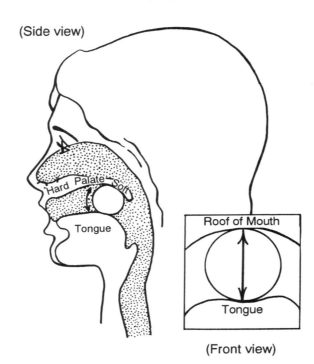

Humming brings the upper resonances into play. The imaginary ball opens the throat and allows the top of the voice to mix with the bottom colors of the voice.

When you finish humming the scales, go through them again. This time, however, for each pair, follow each hummed scale with a scale on one of the basic vowels: Hum-EE, Hum-EH, Hum-OO, Hum-OH, Hum-AH. As you sing each vowel, it should contain the feeling of the hum inside, as if you were humming with your mouth open.

<Musical Example of the Double 5-Note Scale>

EXERCISE #9: FIVE 5-NOTE SCALES

Sing each vowel in order, using one breath for the whole exercise. Be sure to pace yourself: This is where you begin the work to stretch your breath capacity and to sustain tone. Give out your air, keeping in mind how many notes you're about to sing on one breath. You don't want to exhaust yourself before you're done.

<Musical Example of Five 5-Note Scales Exercise>

EXERCISE #10: 9-NOTE SCALES

This exercise will build your coordination. Sing each scale back, up, and over along the pathway, keeping the mouth full of tone, on the way up (and down as well). Focus through the imaginary hole-in-the-wall. Drop your jaw, keeping your mouth oval. Breathe into, and squeeze from, your lower support system. Sing from the bottom of your throat to the corners of your cheekbones, with all tones comfortably filling and being balanced in the mouth. Use AH or one of the other basic vowels.

<Musical Example of the 9-Note Scale Exercise>

EXERCISE #11: ARPEGGIO WITH TURN ON TOP

Here's an exercise to get you to think faster. It's also great for building flexibility into the voice. Try a different vowel on each repetition, as you ascend by leaps and bounds. And be sure to get a good, low breath between each repetition. Make each note of the turn (i.e., one note down, followed by two notes up) count.

<Musical Example of Arpeggio With Turn on Top>

THE SECONDARY VOWELS

It's important to begin including a wider spectrum of vowel sounds to the exercises. Thus far, we have used the five basic or primary vowels. But there are other sounds of the English language to become familiar with in terms of their feel and position in the mouth, throat, and head resonators. This additional group of sounds is known as the secondary vowels.

There are a total of ten vowels that cover nearly all the sounds you will encounter when breaking down words to find just what sound you might be singing at any one time.

As all these new sounds are open, as opposed to the constrictive vowels OO and EE, they follow all the same rules of normal tone production detailed up to this point.

Simply maintain to the best of your ability the directions given in the chapter on the five basic vowels. If you seek focus, anchoring, and gentle initiations, these sounds will fall comfortably into place along with the already familiar basic five. Use this vowel chart to make sure you're pronouncing the vowels correctly in all of the exercises contained in this book.

VOWEL PRONUNCIATION GUIDE

Vowel	As In:	Vowel	As In:
EE	meet	UH	love
EH	bet	ŬH	put*
OO	moon	ĂH	cat*
OH	boat	IH	sit
AH	father	AW	saw

*Throughout this book the vowel sounds found in the words "put" and "cat" will be represented by the symbols ŬH and ĂH respectively.

CHAPTER 11
BLENDING VOCAL COLORS

"It may be stated that, in a certain sense, for every note of the human voice. . . there is a condition of the mechanism of the instrument which is appropriate to this, and to no other note."

William Shakespeare
Voice Instructor and Author
The Art of Singing, 1893

THE TWO PRIMARY VOCAL COLORS - *HEAD RESONANCE AND CHEST RESONANCE*

Although we talked about head and chest resonance to some extent in Chapter 7, there is so much confusion surrounding this matter, balancing brilliance and depth of resonance deserves a more in-depth discussion. If you've ever taken a voice lesson, most likely you've heard the terms "head resonance" and "chest resonance." Blending these two vocal qualities or colors is a major source of confusion and frustration for many, if not most, vocal students. But when you understand how the voice works, blending vocal colors should become as easy and automatic as speaking expressively.

HEAD RESONANCE

It's been established that **head resonance**, when *well-supported*, has a brilliant, ringing tone quality compared to throat and chest resonance. It is developed in the bones and cavities above, behind and around the nose - in the *mask*. As mentioned in the Focus Chapter, mask resonance is one of the most important elements of your sound.

The result of *unsupported* head resonance is very different and is characterized by a false voice or falsetto tone. This is the odd quality that occurs when a singer suddenly switches into a "choir-boy" quality when blend is mismanaged.

As indicated in Appendix 3, The Resonators, your bone structure has a lot to do with what your voice sounds like. It's what makes your voice different than anyone else's. And that's why you can listen to ten singers with high voices, and each will have a very different sound. The difference is due largely to the unique characteristics of every singer's bone structure.

LOCATING HEAD RESONANCE

A simple experiment will allow you to feel and hear the capacity of the resonating system of the head. First, gently tap your finger on the bone beneath your upper lip (photo #11.1 a). Can you hear the thud that your finger makes as it taps the bone? Now tap on the bridge of your nose in the same way (photo #11.2 b). Finally, tap on your forehead at the level of your hairline (photo #11.3 c), again listening for the characteristic thud of that area.

What did you notice about the pitch of the taps at each level? The thuds were higher in pitch as you ascended from the lip to the forehead. By performing this simple experiment, you can hear how certain bones of the head are predisposed to amplify various pitch levels.

PHOTO #11.1 (a) (b) (c) - Finding Head Resonance

a)   b)   c)

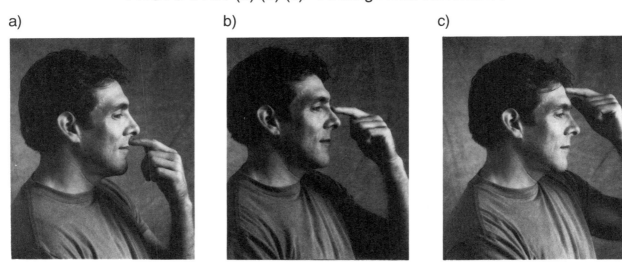

THROAT RESONANCE AND CHEST RESONANCE

When singers refer to *"chest resonance,"* they're talking about tone which is characterized by darker vowel qualities or mellowness. However, the term "chest resonance" is misleading. By definition, an effective resonating chamber is a hollow place surrounded by hard surfaces. The chest is too full of organs (heart, lungs, etc.), to be suitable for amplifying tone.

WHERE EXACTLY DOES THROAT AND CHEST RESONANCE OCCUR?

Where there *is* plenty of empty space for amplification of the lower vibrations created by the vocal cords, however, is in the mouth and throat (as previously stated, lower resonance or depth of tone is to be known as throat/chest resonance in these pages). *Most* so-called "chest resonance" really comes from the throat. However, there's also a distinct sensation of vibration in the chest when singing, especially in the area of the sternum, or breastbone (see Illustration #11.1). As previously noted, this feel of tone gathering in the chest area can be used very effectively to stabilize high notes (see double-anchoring, Chapter 7).

ILLUSTRATION #11.1 - Location of Throat and Chest Resonance

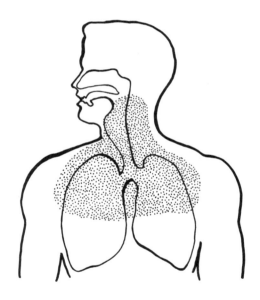

It's as if you have two mirrors that reflect what's happening at the level of the cords. One mirror is the vibration you feel in the bones and cavities of the head; this is the sensation referred to in these pages as "focus". The other is the vibration felt lower, in the throat/chest area; this commonly is referred to as "chest resonance." Both mirrors work together to reflect and amplify the tone originated in the cords and bones of the surrounding voice box. In other words, these parts of the instrument vibrate *sympathetically* with the sound given off by the cords (see Illustration #11.2).

ILLUSTRATION #11.2 - Two Mirrors
Reflecting Vibration Originating At The Cords

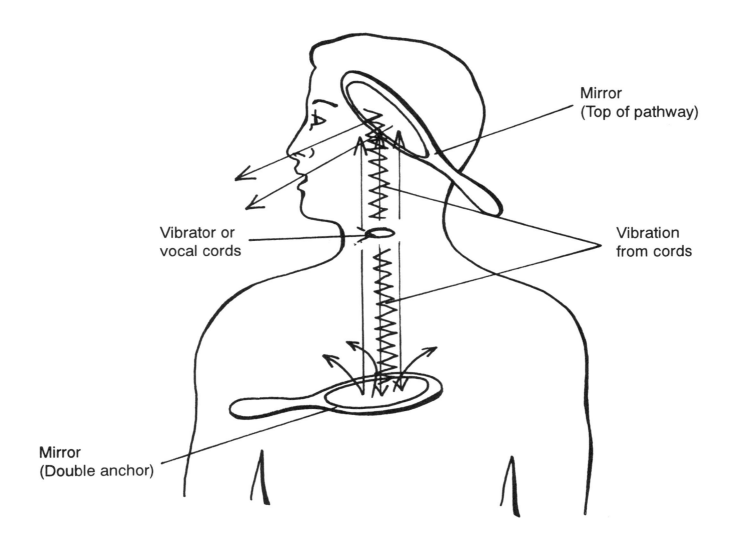

Mirror
(Top of pathway)

Vibration
from cords

Vibrator or
vocal cords

Mirror
(Double anchor)

THE EFFECT OF SYMPATHETIC VIBRATION

You've experienced **sympathetic vibration** if you've heard and felt what happens when a car with a loud stereo drives by. You don't just hear the initial vibration of sound; you also get sympathetic vibration - the windows of your house shake, the pictures on the wall rattle. Another example of sympathetic vibration is the stereotypical image of an opera singer breaking a glass when singing a very high note.

When you're singing, both areas - the upper (head) and the lower (throat/chest) resonators vibrate sympathetically with the vibration of the cords. The bones and hollows that make up these resonators, though, do not *make* vibration; they pick up the vibration of the cords and produce sympathetic vibration.

THE RELATIONSHIP BETWEEN HEAD AND THROAT/CHEST RESONANCE

It's important to realize that the upper and lower resonances (brilliance and depth) are completely wedded to each other. ***Never attempt to take them apart;*** instead, allow the appropriate blend of head and throat/chest resonance to combine in the mouth - the place the two qualities are mixed. When tone is anchored in the mouth, it's also automatically blended.

USING IMAGERY TO BLEND THE VOICE

The Lever and the Fulcrum

A good way to visualize the blending of tone is to think of a lever and fulcrum, or "teeter-totter" (see Illustration #11.3). The following description shows how the voice naturally produces high or low tone in response to our urge to sing in either range. Later in this chapter, the all important process of blending (whereby singers complete tones at the top or bottom of their voices with the opposite resonance will be discussed).

ILLUSTRATION #11.3 - The Lever and the Fulcrum of the Voice

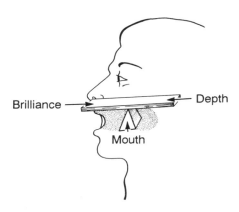

In this analogy, the fulcrum is the mouth, full of vowel (the anchor), and the lever is tipped forward into head or back into throat/chest resonance, depending on the type of sound desired.

As long as the fulcrum is holding up the lever, you're okay. When your mouth is full of the vowel sound you're singing, you can lean towards the head resonators, or you can let the tone tilt back into the throat resonators.

For tones requiring more brilliance, mentally lean the lever forward into the bones and cavities of the mask (see Illustration #11.4).

ILLUSTRATION #11.4 - Lever and Fulcrum:
Leaning Toward Head Resonance

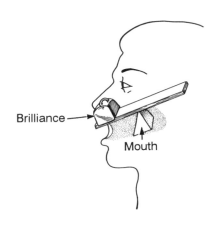

Tones of darker character will cause the imaginary teeter-totter to drop in the rear (see Illustration #11.5).

ILLUSTRATION #11.5 - The Lever and the Fulcrum:
Leaning Back into Throat Resonance

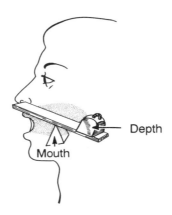

Singers get into trouble when they forget about the balance between the resonators. If your mouth is full of vowel, you won't have to think about how much head (or throat) resonance you have. You'll always have the required amount of throat resonance, even in the highest tones, and enough head resonance in the lowest tones.

If your mouth feels empty, as if you're singing above or below it, your tone will have a one-dimensional quality that's unpleasant to listeners.

In other words, if you only seek resonance in the head and attempt to divorce yourself from the sensation in your mouth, throat, and chest, the tones don't settle or have weight. Your tone will lack the capacity to express feelings other than the gentler emotions. So you lose half of your expressive palette if you consistently sing primarily in purified head resonance.

Conversely, if your tone isn't hooked up into the bones and cavities of the head strongly enough, the whole voice is likely to fall down into the throat when you attempt to add throat/chest resonance. In this case, when required to sing with conviction, the vocal response will be watered-down at best.

A key to blending is to always keep the mouth full of vowel, or anchored. As long as you can feel the vibration in your mouth, you can lean as far forward into the mask as you like, or as far back and down into the throat/chest. The mouth receives tone from both resonators and anchors it, giving it the balance required for truly expressive singing.

WHAT HAPPENS IF YOU TRY TO SEPARATE HEAD AND THROAT RESONANCE?

Here's what happens if you try to separate upper and lower resonance: when you're singing notes in throat/chest resonance and you suddenly switch to head resonance, your voice cracks. This situation is much too familiar for many singers. To alleviate this problem, the trick is to learn to blend upper and lower resonance. *This blending of vocal colors must exist absolutely in the mind first of all.* Only then can you reasonably expect the instrument to mix tones naturally, without effort.

TWO OR THREE REGISTERS?

Exactly how do you achieve this blending of head and throat resonance? There are a number of different theories as to how this is done. Most commonly taught are the two and three register systems. Unfortunately, they both are more trouble than they're worth.

The following descriptions of the two and three register systems will help you to understand what approach to blending you're currently using. Afterwards, the best solution to the problem - the **one register system** will be fully explained.

THE TWO REGISTER SYSTEM

Using this system, the idea is that as you sing from the bottom of your range to the top, your voice can comfortably sing through a group of notes known as the chest register without any physical adjustments to the vocal cords in the voice box. *(A **register** is said to be any group of notes that can be sung with the same physical setting of the cords in terms of length, thickness and tightness.)*

The Dreaded Crack or "Break"

Then, suddenly, at a particular pitch, the voice "cracks" or "breaks"! In order to sing into the head register (or notes above the crack), you must then make a physical adjustment with which all the higher notes may be sung.

In the two register technique, this "break" is where your chest voice ends and your head voice begins (see Illustration #11.6). In this system, much worry and perspiration is spent trying to "conceal" the break.

ILLUSTRATION #11.6 - The Two Register System

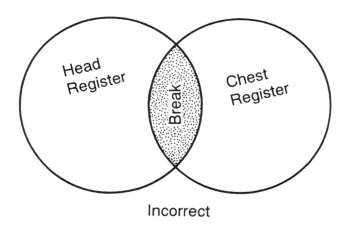

Incorrect

THREE REGISTERS: EVEN MORE DIFFICULT THAN TWO!

Another popular way of teaching blending resonances divides the voice into *three* separate registers: low, middle, and high. In this system, the idea is that there is an additional middle group of notes (or register) which consists of a separate setting of the vocal cords for the transition notes between the head and throat registers (see Illustration #11.7 below).

ILLUSTRATION #11.7 - The Three Register System

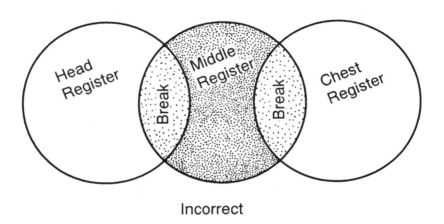

Incorrect

The Two and Three Register Systems <u>*Create*</u> *Fear*

Mechanically, the two and three register systems are fairly good models of the inner workings of the voice. To sing throughout the range of your voice does, in fact, require small muscular adjustments to the voice box and vocal cords.

Psychologically, however, these techniques *create* fear, rather than alleviate it. Singers trained in these methods usually dread singing any notes in and around their "break." Anticipation and fear of cracking are far more dangerous than the actual adjustments required to avoid it.

ONE REGISTER

Shifting to a more helpful model should solve the registration problem once and for all. First, think of a piano: each key is attached to a hammer, which is poised to strike a string which produces a particular note or tone. For every key, there's a separate string which is preset at a particular length, thickness, and tightness.

No two notes share a common string. If you play a group of five notes that ascend higher and higher in pitch, you will have caused five different strings, with five different settings of length, thickness, and tightness, to vibrate.

EVERY NOTE HAS IT'S OWN UNIQUE SETTING OF THE CORDS

The voice functions the same way as the piano! If you sing any two different notes, the vocal cords must change their length, thickness and tightness to create the correct pitch for each note. With the voice, too, each note has it's own unique setting of the cords, EVERY NOTE IS ITS OWN REGISTER! Each time you sing a note that differs from a previous note, you're *automatically* making adjustments. It doesn't make sense to divide the voice arbitrarily into two (or three) parts. The voice can adjust the relationship between head and chest resonance or shift gears, so to speak, on different notes, vowels, and volume levels automatically if you'll let it.

If It's Not Broken, Don't Fix It!

It's much easier, and the results are far better, when you allow the voice itself to gauge and control the blending of the upper and lower resonances, or registers. The voice tends to crack in the places that you're *afraid* it will crack or when you try to artificially make physical adjustments to achieve head or throat resonance.

Many singers who have a terrible time "adjusting registers" become free of this bothersome problem as soon as the voice is thought of as one long connected span of tones. Each tone blends upper and lower colors, head and throat/chest resonance automatically. Forcing the voice to shift gears is like driving a stick-shift compared to an automatic transmission where you simply allow the instrument to adjust internally.

YIN YANG: COMBINING HEAD, CHEST AND THROAT RESONANCE

To easily combine head and throat/chest resonance, it's helpful to think of the symbol used for one aspect of Eastern philosophy known as Yin-Yang (see Illustration #11.8).

ILLUSTRATION #11.8 - Yin-Yang: The One Register System

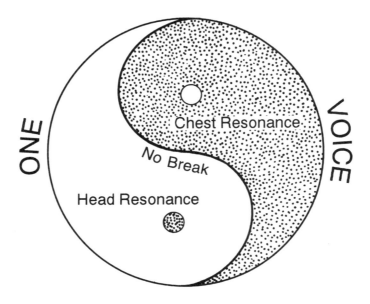

Yin-Yang deals with the duality of opposites. Everything in life has an opposite character, e.g., male and female, fire and water, night and day, etc. Think of the voice in
this way: the throat/chest resonance as the dark part of the Yin-Yang symbol with
the light part of the symbol representing head resonance.

HEAD + THROAT RESONANCE = A <u>WHOLE</u> VOICE

Notice that each section within the outer perimeter contains a part of the other and
both make up the whole voice. And there's no crack in this model, because the
voice is represented by the outer perimeter that is wrapped around both qualities. If
you're singing higher or softer notes, the balance is simply shifted towards the
lighter side of the symbol (see Illustration #11.9).

High tones will naturally be felt to vibrate in the head resonators. To add
just the right touch of depth (throat/chest resonance) for balance, imagine
pressing some of the air onto the backside of your breastbone (sternum).
The Yin-Yang concept works because the two major vocal colors, brilliance
and depth, are enhanced by the presence of each other. There's always a
bit of light in the dark portion of the circle and vice-versa.

ILLUSTRATION #11.9 - Yin-Yang: Shifting
Towards Head Resonance for Soft and High Notes

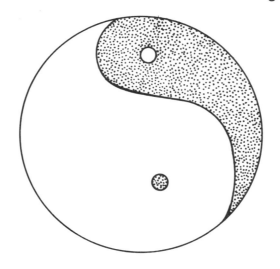

When singing louder or lower, the balance shifts towards the darker side of the symbol (see Illustration #11.10). It's what you intend to sing in terms of volume, feeling and pitch (usually determined by the emotions a song obligates you to sing about) that causes the change to occur by itself. You don't have to do it. When singing low notes which automatically resonate in the throat/chest, be sure to feel for some vibration in the cheek bones, behind the nose and in the forehead. Color the deeper tones with enough mask resonance to keep them ringing and from becoming bottom heavy.

ILLUSTRATION #11.10 -
Yin-Yang: Shifting Towards Throat/Chest Resonance for Loud or Low Notes

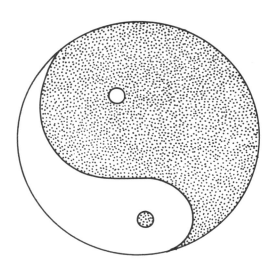

It doesn't matter whether you're singing high, low, loud or soft, you're *always* singing with a *blend* of head and throat resonance. And this blend is, naturally and simply, mixed in the mouth as long as the voice stays *anchored* and breath is evenly supported and controlled.

SINGING IS SLOW MOTION SPEECH

If you doubt the voice's ability to blend these tonal qualities automatically, think how many vocal colors are used in common speech throughout the day.

Unless one speaks consistently in a monotone voice, there are hundreds of vocal tone variations used each day, just in ordinary conversation! But do you worry about breaks, registers, or upper or lower resonance while telling an exciting story or explaining a detailed experience to someone? Never!

For example, if you were calling out to someone in the distance, you'd undoubtedly let out a roaring yell that was a wonderful blend of brilliant head and deep throat/chest resonance. Yet, if you talked a tired baby to sleep, the dominant quality of your voice would be a light head resonance. And it's all done without conscious help. Similarly, singing is basically slow motion speech with more or less intensity depending on the emotional obligation of the lyric.

PLACEMENT: A MEANS OF EXPRESSION

Placement is one of those musical terms just vague enough to be confusing. What it actually describes is this balance of sympathetic resonance that occurs in the lower and upper resonators that has been discussed in this chapter. If tone is emphasizing upper resonance, we say the voice is "placed" high and/or forward. On the other hand, if throat/chest resonators are mostly coloring the tone, placement is said to be "low," "down," or even sometimes "further back."

This relates to the fulcrum/lever analogy. Leaned forward, the voice is also said to be placed forward. And the same goes for leaning or placing the voice to the "back" in the throat.

Where you choose to emphasize or concentrate the energy of the voice depends on what mood you want to convey. Placement is one of the key ingredients of expression. It gives variety to your singing.

HOW TO CREATE A MOOD BY PLACING YOUR VOICE

Though an oversimplification, you could say that to express a happy, excited feeling, you would place the voice by leaning it more into head resonance. Darker, somber moods are revealed by placing or aiming the tone more in the direction of the throat or chest (see Illustration #11.11).

The key is to remember that it must always go, to some degree, in both directions at once, and still be anchored in the mouth. A subtle emphasis into either head or throat/chest resonance is all that's necessary to infuse the voice with all the various emotional colors at your command.

ILLUSTRATION #11.11 -
Placing the Voice to Convey Specific Feelings

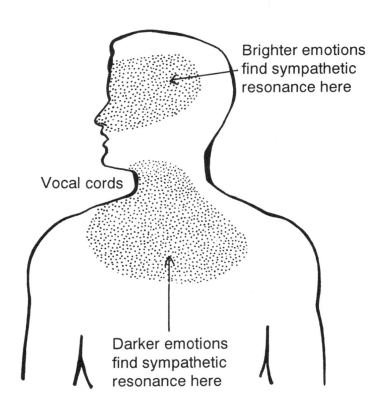

THE EASY WAY TO BLEND: JUST LET IT HAPPEN!

All of these adjustments occur automatically, just by knowing the quality of sound you want to make. *Again, as a singer, you must learn to move your mind (i.e, imagine what you want your sound to be) before you move your mouth!*

If you consistently practice and master the basics so that anchoring, breathing, pathway, focus and mouth position work together, blending of the registers takes care of itself. This is especially true if you have your emotional intention clearly in mind before you start singing a song.

CHAPTER 12

THE ULTIMATE
VOCAL WORK-OUT
(MESSA di VOCE)

*"If I don't practice one day, I know it; two days, the critics know it;
three days, the public knows it."*

Jascha Heifetz

EXERCISE #12: THE <u>BEST</u> BLEND EXERCISE

Some exercises are better than others for learning to blend the head and throat/chest qualities. The best blend exercise ever developed is undoubtedly the one historically known as **Messa di Voce**. The term literally means "setup of the voice." By doing this exercise, you take an inventory of how the different parts of the voice are strengthening and integrating.

MESSA di VOCE IS THE HIGHEST TECHNICAL ACHIEVEMENT IN THE ART OF SINGING

No other exercise requires a more complete or perfect combination of breath support, focus and anchoring. At first glance, it's deceptively simple. Messa di Voce is basically just taking a note and gradually adjusting the volume over about 20 seconds.

The challenge is in doing the exercise without a loss of basic tone quality. The voice should remain steady and even, without a bump between the louder and softer portions of the sound. The ability to do this on a *steady* stream of air is essential to good singing.

Be Patient!

When you first try this exercise, it might feel a bit like the first time you drove a car. Remember how overwhelming that was? Not only did you have to steer the car, manage the speed, gauge for when to brake, etc., but you also had to watch for oncoming traffic while staying in your lane. Now, however, driving is a piece of cake for most of us. Careful practice of the Messa di Voce will give you the same sense of confidence in your singing.

GETTING RID OF THE "BREAK"

What *exactly* does Messa di Voce do for you? It joins the mouth/throat and head resonances of the voice, eliminating the "break" that can occur as you sing into the higher range of the voice.

The tone quality you achieve while performing this exercise is an accurate gauge of your current blending ability. As you improve your capacity to combine the depth and brilliance in your voice smoothly and consistently, this exercise will keep the vocal blending muscles well-practiced and conditioned.

ONE TONE AT A TIME

When practicing the Messa di Voce, always work on one tone at a time. At the beginning, pick a tone which is in the middle of your voice. The initial tone should *not* be in head resonance, or what many people call "falsetto."

To find a good note to start on, just sing any tone that doesn't feel particularly high or low. Use a tone quality that is not whispered or yelly, but is a solid blend, both ringing and full-throated. Check your CD for examples of how each version of the BEST BLEND (MESSA di VOCE) exercise should ideally sound.

HERE'S HOW TO DO IT:

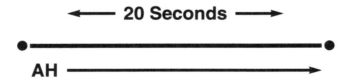

It will help to do a simplified version of the Messa di Voce first. Simply sustain an AH vowel for twenty seconds at medium volume. That's all! Pick a note in the middle of your voice, check your watch for your start time, take a quiet, low breath and spin out a medium volume tone for twenty seconds.

If this is difficult, you'll need to improve your breath control and support by stepping up your work on the Controlled Release exercise. When you can hold a tone for twenty seconds without any difficulty, you're ready to move on to the more advanced forms of the exercise.

<Musical Example #3: The Loud-Soft-Loud Version>

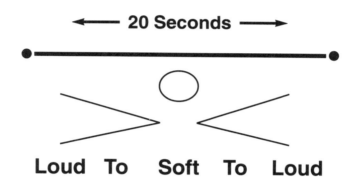

Now you're ready for the second version of the best blend exercise. Here's how it goes. Once again, select a tone in the middle of your voice, not high and not too low, and get ready to sustain it for twenty seconds. You'll find sample starting notes on your CD. Keep the tone well-anchored at all times.

Begin singing the tone at medium loud volume (not blasting!) and slowly soften the tone gradually until it is as soft as you can sing it - without changing into a completely falsetto sound. This gradual softening should take ten seconds. Without interruption, gradually increase the volume over the next ten seconds. Whether the voice is shifting towards soft or loud resonance, *always* keep your mouth full of tone (the AH vowel, that is).

Don't be surprised if all sorts of strange cracks, breaks, bumps and pitch fluctuations occur as you try to steadily move from a loud to a soft and then to a loud tone again. This is normal at first. Remember, the Messa di Voce is a long-term exercise and will improve markedly only after much effort has been enlisted to the cause. But every little improvement in the quality of this important exercise will result in major improvements in your ability to control your blend while singing. It's definitely worth the effort.

<Musical Example #4: The Soft-Loud-Soft Version>

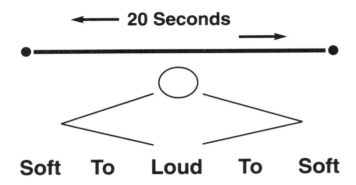

This is the most advanced version of the Messa di Voce work. However, if you've prepared by doing the warm-up and loud-soft-loud versions, as just described, you'll be well on your way to mastering the soft-loud-soft version. Begin singing a tone as near in volume to a whisper as possible. Very gradually, swell the tone for ten seconds until you're singing very loudly (but just less than your loudest).

Don't forget, in order to get the benefits of this exercise, it's essential that the tone is anchored and supported. As you begin, focus while simultaneously feeling for vibration resonating in the throat/chest cavity. In all versions of this best blend exercise, steady the tone by gently continuing the internal (muscular) motions of inhalation while singing. As volume increases and decreases, use the reversed megaphone image to help stabilize tone. Imagine the pathway moving through a megaphone which slants forward to the point of focus *at the same angle for all volume levels.*

KEEP THE TONE SMOOTH!

Now for the most challenging part. At the ten second mark, begin decreasing volume gradually over another ten seconds until you're at a whisper again. The objective is to keep the tone smooth throughout and to achieve the most dramatic extremes in volume that you can. Start as soft as you can, swell (crescendo) as loud as you can, and then the softer you sing in the final decrescendo (softening of tone), the better. Keep the tone as steady and pleasing as possible throughout the twenty seconds.

REMEMBER TO BLEND!

On the soft portions of the soft-loud-soft blend exercise (the very beginning and the end), be sure to sustain just a bit of chest resonance. It's impossible to avoid cracking as you get louder (or softer) if you're not blending head and throat/chest resonance throughout the entire twenty seconds of any repetition of this exercise.

Without the presence of both qualities, tension is transferred too rapidly from one point on the cords to another, resulting in dramatic shifts between head and throat/chest resonance. These awkward changes of balance (the bumps and waverings in the tone) will disappear as your ability to blend improves.

REPETITION IS THE KEY TO SUCCESS

If you have trouble with the Messa di Voce in the beginning, don't despair. Just doing the exercise over and over again will produce the smoothness, subtle volume changes and blend that characterize this exercise in its finished state. Again, be assured that perfecting these Messa di Voce exercises takes a good many weeks or months, even under the best circumstances.

THE THIRTY SECOND MESSA di VOCE

When you reach the point where performing the Messa di Voce over a twenty second period is a piece of cake, add five seconds to each half of the exercise. You'll discover even more delicate refinements occurring throughout your performances of songs and other exercises when you've mastered the thirty second version of Messa di Voce. That's the power of this exercise: it touches on many aspects of singing: breath support, breath control, pathway, focus, anchoring, and blend. *There's really nothing you can do that will improve your voice more than mastering Messa di Voce!*

PART TWO:
THE UPPER VOICE

CHAPTER 13

COUNTERBALANCING AND THE SINGER'S POINT OF VIEW

"All artful singing is conceptual. A singer cannot possibly sing a pitch without first conceiving it as sensation."

D. Ralph Appelman
The Science of Vocal Pedagogy

SINGING: ART OR SCIENCE?

Singers and other artists often play up the mysterious aspect of their art. The attitude is that it's something you're either born with or you're not. While some people acquire the skills of singing more readily than others (and some people work harder than others), unless you're tone deaf, you *can* learn to sing.

This attitude is especially prevalent concerning singing in the upper range. Many singers who have beautiful voices shy away from singing in the upper extension because they feel they weren't born with the ability to sing high notes.

They think that singers who have great top notes must have always had them. While it's true that it may come easier for some, it's also true that most singers with sturdy top notes probably practiced endless hours to achieve such strength and control in the upper ranges.

Don't get discouraged by the myth that successful singers are born singers. Although great singing sometimes occurs because of the singer's natural talent, many (if not *most*) great vocal artists acquired their abilities through tireless study, practice, as well as experience on the stage and in the studio.

If you consistently practice the basics, your range *will* grow. Never limit yourself to what you *think* you can do; instead, do your best, practicing all of the secrets contained in this book, and *discover* your real vocal potential.

DON'T HIDE FROM "HIGH NOTES"

There's one question that's asked by almost every student of singing: "How can I sing high notes without straining my voice or having the tone sound shrill and harsh?" The answer is very simple if you've mastered the Secrets of Singing: You'll find that *there's no such thing as a "high" note!*

Everything you've learned so far about singing applies to *every note* in your range. A note at the top end of your voice needs the same consistent attention to technical detail as any other note. Thinking a top note through the pathway, supporting with a low breath, and keeping the jaw loose and low so it can anchor comfortably in the mouth, will take the high out of any "high" note. As the tone balances and finds its place among your resonators, you'll feel the fight go out of it.

Notes in the upper part of your range will come within reach as the timing of your abdominal and rib muscles coordinate better with the diaphragm in sending air to the cords at the precise moment and required degree of intensity.

Don't weaken your ability to sing in your upper range by giving it any special significance!

PREPARING FOR THE UPPER RANGE

Singing notes in the upper extension (or in *any* range) is just like taking a test. If you've prepared adequately for the test, you may have a few jitters, but for the most part, you'll feel confident that you'll be able to perform well on the test.

On the other hand, if you've waited until the last minute to "cram" (or if you're hoping the test will be multiple choice, so that you'll have a good shot at guessing the answers) you're going to be extremely nervous about it.

This is the way many singers approach singing in the upper extension: they hope and pray that they'll hit the "high" note, but they're not so sure that it's really going to happen. The whole song fades into the background while the singer anxiously awaits the "high" notes.

It's important to know that singing in the upper extension is not multiple choice. You can't guess or hope that the note will be there. *You have to do your homework* (i.e., practicing the breath work, making sure your placement is correct, keeping your instrument relaxed, etc.). *Then* you can relax and enjoy singing the whole song, knowing that *every* note will be imbued with richness, fullness and ease.

P.O.V.
IT ALL DEPENDS ON HOW YOU SEE IT

P.O.V. is a term taken from the film world which stands for *Point of View (P.O.V.)*. When singing one or a series of lofty tones, approach them mentally from above and behind (see Illustration #13.1). The higher you sing, the more this vantage point becomes critical. By approaching difficult notes and passages this way, you'll be in a better position to practice the professional's habit of *counterbalancing*. Counterbalancing is the sum total of all efforts to keep the breath, focus, jaw, and tongue from lifting as you approach a tone in the upper range.

Nothing sets the stage better than imagining that all top notes (in fact, all notes of the voice from the middle on up) are approached from above and behind. (In terms of the reversed megaphone described in Chapter 6, the back end of the megaphone grows taller as the pitches you sing get higher.) One aims the voice from above and behind the megaphone, straight down and out along the pathway through the hole-in-the-wall. Be sure to add plenty of resist with the diaphragm; and double-anchor every top note by filling the mouth with vowel and leaning air onto the inside wall of the chest for balance. This in a nutshell is your counterweight to the soaring top notes of the voice.

ILLUSTRATION #13.1 - P.O.V.:
Initiating a Tone From Above and Behind

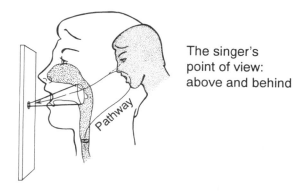

The singer's
point of view:
above and behind

A TONE IS A TONE:
NO MORE, NO LESS

Low, middle, *and "high"* tones all have to anchor and exit through the mouth. Additionally, some air exits through the nose. But whatever tone you choose, ("high," middle, or low), the air *always* begins at the lower breath support system and *always* exits through the mouth and the nose. From this perspective, you can see that there's really nothing special about a "high" note.

If you had a hole in your forehead, and could only sing a "high" note if you moved it out through that hole, then you'd probably have quite a bit of difficulty producing "high" notes. *But you don't.* To produce clear, ringing "high" notes, you only need to remember the basics of good tone production: maintain good breath support and control, keep the tongue and jaw relaxed and low, and keep a focused mouth position. In a word, *counterbalance.* When you achieve this combination of physical factors, all "high" notes will feel as easy as the middle notes. *Remember, what you think is how you sing.*

This is especially true when singing notes that leap to a high note or when starting a phrase on a high pitch. By aiming top notes down and out along the pathway, [from an elevated Point of View, above and behind the pathway (see Illustration #13.1)], they stay firmly in the mouth and focused. This practice will stop the tendency to reach (literally crane your head and neck up) for top tones. It will also prevent you from smacking top notes with too much air.

EXERCISE #13 - INITIATE A TONE,
LEAP AN OCTAVE, TWO TURNS, DOWN A SCALE

After starting the exercise, move to the top note, lifting the tone and dropping down into place from above and behind (from a good Point of View). Then add two turns for flexibility (stay above and behind) and then sing down the scale.

As you sing to the top note, keep in mind the five elements of counterbalancing:

1. Aim down (through the hole-in-the-wall)
2. Keep the tongue down and touching the bottom-front teeth
3. The jaw drops down
4. Breath must be (controlled) by a resisting diaphragm
5. A little throat/chest resonance (double-anchor) is added to balance the natural mask resonance of the upper range

<Musical Example: Initiate a Tone, Leap an Octave, Two Turns, Down a Scale>

Exercise 13

Version 1: Ah ⎯⎯⎯⎯⎯⎯⎯⎯⎯⎯⎯⎯⎯⎯⎯⎯

etc.

CHAPTER 14

PENULTIMATES

"Fear or stage fright finds an antidote in the courage acquired from the knowledge of possessing a sound technique."

E. Herbert Caesari

PREPARATION NOTES:
SET YOURSELF UP FOR SUCCESS

After you've rehearsed a song and identified the notes that are above your normal speech level, it's important to examine the notes leading up to these so-called "high notes." For example, the last phrase from the chorus in the ballad "You Are the Sunshine of My Life" (Stevie Wonder, 1972 Jobete Music Co., Inc.) leads up to a "high" note (SEE EXCERPT) on the word "my":

<Musical Example #5>

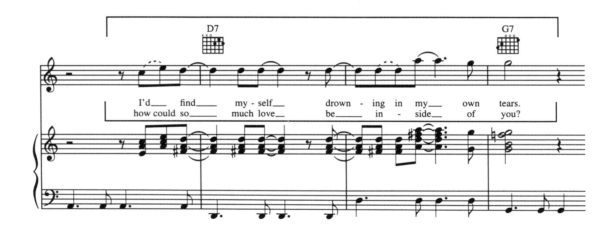

The sung tones for the words "Drowning in..." lead up to a top A natural (on the word "my") in the music. Without proper preparation, this phrase can be problematic to say the least. Most singers will gloss over the first three notes, anxiously anticipating the top note. However, these tones, called **penultimate** tones (literally, meaning the next to the last notes, from the Latin paene=almost and ultimus=last), are really *more* important than the "high" note. It's the notes that come before the peak of the phrase that give you the opportunity to prepare for the top note.

<Musical Example #6>

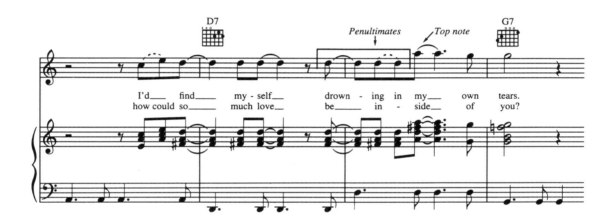

PENULTIMATE CHECKLIST

Here's a checklist to refer to when you're preparing to sing in your upper range. When practicing any note or a series of notes leading up to a climactic top note, make sure:

    ✔   the entire body is relaxed

    ✔   the breath is low

    ✔   there's the sensation of the beginning of a yawn set up when taking a breath and that it remains in place throughout the singing of the upcoming phrase

    ✔   there's the correct amount of breath support (gentle pressing instead of pushing air to the cords)

    ✔   the tongue and jaw are relaxed and properly positioned

    ✔   the voice is focused (the front end of the reversed megaphone is mentally in place)

    ✔   the voice has the freedom to seek depth and brilliance simultaneously (that is, it feels like you're singing from the mask, mouth and chest; or focused and double-anchored, at the same time)

    ✔   there's no hesitation leading up to the top note

    ✔   the top note is approached from above and behind (the P.O.V. is down)

●   This may seem like a lot of things to keep in mind when singing. That's where the exercises come in. If you've been practicing them regularly, it should be evident that many of the requirements listed above happen naturally by now. Keeping one or two vocal ideas in mind is probably all that's required. Eventually, your practicing will bury all the techniques of this book deep in your bones and muscles, leaving your instrument open to the images and emotions of the songs you'll be singing.

TOP NOTES ARE REALLY ANTI-CLIMACTIC

If you sing the penultimate notes correctly, you don't need to give much thought to any "high" note. Powerful, open top notes will be a natural result of your preparation. And that's the way it should be. Any effort to fix mouth shape, change tongue position, adjust airflow, etc., when you're singing a top note is woefully too late. Doing that will only cause tension while you nervously struggle to adjust the "high" note.

Just making sure that all the ingredients of great singing are contained in the penultimates will allow top notes to take care of themselves. Also be certain that you don't rush a top note or sing to it or at it. Sing *through* upper notes, recognizing that they work just like tones in the low and middle parts of the voice.

EXERCISE #14: THREE DESCENDING TONES, OCTAVE JUMP, HOLD FOR THREE COUNTS

Here's an opportunity to practice counterbalancing, P.O.V., and penultimates all together. For this exercise, sing down a three-note scale, then leap an octave and hold a note above for three counts. The three descending notes will serve as your penultimates for the top note. Check all your instrumental factors in the three notes before you leap and make sure you sing from above and behind to the upper range. Be sure to counterbalance, keeping everything (jaw, breath, tongue, etc.) low.

<Musical Example of Three Tones, Octave Jump, with Three Count Hold>

Exercise 14

Version 1: Ah _____

CHAPTER 15
VOWEL MODIFICATIONS

"The beauty of the voice and the expression of emotion is heard in the vowel sounds, the intensity and colour of which can be varied to a very great extent."

Arnold Rose
The Singer and The Voice

THE "ALL-NATURAL" INGREDIENT

If changing your point of view and preparing the penultimate notes still hasn't made upper range singing comfortable, the advanced vowel work in this chapter will.

There is an often overlooked natural process that occurs in the voice, when singing in the upper extension, that makes it easier to sing "high" notes and creates a pleasant rounded tone. The procedure is known as **vowel modification**.

A vowel modification is any intentional slight adjustment to the sound of a vowel, with the goal of attaining more comfortable and pleasing tone production. Although this operation may occur naturally, sometimes singers resist the natural tendencies of the voice, making it necessary to re-learn the subtleties of singing vowels in the upper extension.

*When you learn to follow what your instrument is telling you, you're likely to wonder "How could it be this **easy** to sing 'high' notes?"*

"DARKENING" YOUR VOWELS CREATES BETTER TONES

The technique of modifying vowels in the upper range "covers" up the unpleasant stridency that characterizes an uncontrolled "high" note. Vowel modification is also referred to as *covering, vowel mutation, and sometimes vowel darkening.*

Don't modify vowels when singing in the lower and middle ranges. Modifying, or "darkening," vowels in these ranges will create a muffled tone.

Singing Shouldn't Be Struggling

In normal comfortable singing, your voice naturally adjusts the relationship between the throat, mouth, and tongue through small vowel modifications as you sing higher and higher. These adjustments are very, very small - it's difficult to express just how delicate they are.

As you sing upward, the pharynx (the inner throat above the cords and behind the tongue) tries to create space to insure an easy flow of air. This is the process that naturally produces very small changes in the tone. The tone will actually become darker, or less "yell-like" as this happens. For some singers, these natural vocal adjustments get overthrown or forgotten, due to poor training or just inventing personal survival techniques.

Darkening vowels helps the voice box resist the tendency to lift up along with the tone. An awareness of these vowel modifications aids the general efforts of counterbalancing. As pitch goes up, everything else must stay *down.* This, of course, includes the voice box (or larynx). By gradually modifying vowel tone a bit darker in upper phrases or on individual top notes, as needed, the larynx is coaxed just a little lower. The stabilized, normal position for the voice box on all well-sung notes, including "high" notes, is known as the **"floating"** position (see Illustration #15.1a).

ILLUSTRATION #15.1 (a) - Position of Larynx
When Singing Vowel Modification (Floating Larynx)

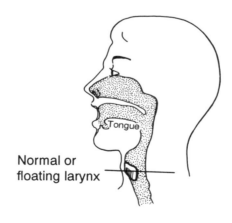

Normal or
floating larynx

Untrained singers resist these natural changes, struggling to sing vowels just like they sound in speech all the way to the top of the voice's range. They try to avoid the natural vowel modifications, thinking that somehow this is "cheating." The end result is the strain that often accompanies the production of "high" notes. Strain and tension usually result as soon as a singer's voice box raises above the floating position or is depressed below it (see Illustrations #15.1b and #15.1c).

ILLUSTRATION #15.1 (b) - Position of Larynx
When Singing Pure Vowel (Raised Larynx)

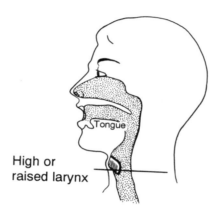

ILLUSTRATION #15.1 (c) - Voice Box Artificially
Depressed to Attain Deeper Sound On Top

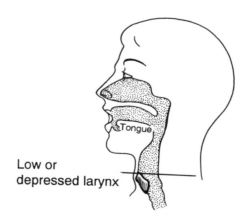

Some teachings advocate forcibly keeping the larynx down to achieve a deeper or richer tone. This only puts the vocal mechanism under excessive stress.

VOWEL MODIFICATIONS SHOULD BE THOUGHT, NOT SUNG

To create vowel modifications, you must learn to *mentally* hear one vowel sound while singing another. By simply thinking about a certain vowel sound, a tiny bit of that vowel sound will blend into the vowel you're actually singing.

When the technique works correctly, you end up with a hybrid vowel. It's a lot like mixing house paint. If you wanted to paint the walls of your home white, but not *glaringly* white, you'd tone down the white paint by adding a few drops of a different color, such as blue. The end result would still be white, but it would be a softer white.

The same applies to vowel modifications: you still want to hear the original vowel, but you want to soften it by adding a hint of another vowel. The effect is very subtle and it takes some practice to discover what proportion of each vowel sound creates the best tone for your particular voice.

Vowel modification can also be thought of as tuning in a radio station on a radio that has a dial tuner; you keep turning the knob back and forth until the station comes in loud, clear, and without any static. Do the same with vowels. At a certain proportion of modification, the tone will be clear and rounded, and you'll be able to sing much more comfortably in the upper extension of your voice.

IH AND ŬH: THE MODIFIERS

Use IH as in "sit," and ŬH as in "put" to darken vowels. Refer to the vowel modification chart below to determine which of the modifiers to use. The vowels in the left column are those sounds typically found making up the lyrics of the songs, arias, and show tunes. The two sounds on the right are the main vowel modifiers. IH, as in the word "sit" is used for the first four sounds on the charts while ŬH, as in "put," is used to modify the last five vowel sounds on the chart. Again, these modifications are to be used in the upper range only.

VOWEL MODIFICATIONS	
PURE VOWEL SOUND	**MODIFIER**
EE as in "m**ee**t"	
EH as in "b**e**t"	
ĂH as in "c**a**t"	**ĬH**
AY as in "d**ay**" (a diphthong, but commonly sung as pure)	(sit)
OO as in "m**oo**n"	
OH as in "b**oa**t"	
AH as in "f**a**ther"	**ŬH**
UH as in "l**o**ve"	(put)
AW as in "s**a**w"	

PRACTICING VOWEL MODIFICATIONS

Iere's how to use the vowel modification chart on the preceding page to make tone adjustments that will greatly benefit your top notes. First, take a "high" note (any note or passage from a song or exercise that feels slightly out of reach or uncomfortable) and sing it on one of the pure vowel sounds, like EE. Notice the quality of the tone. It probably has a "yelly" quality.

Now, sing the same "high" note again, singing on EE, hearing the IH modifier in your imagination. Remember to keep singing EE, and just *think* IH in your mind. Be careful not to allow your mouth to fill with the modification (IH). The result should still sound like EE, but with a softer and rounder tone quality.

You may notice that you feel the modified version of the vowel filling up more of the "back" of the mouth. This is exactly as it should be. A modification literally creates a small amount of extra space in the back of the mouth. That's what allows for the full, rounded tone of a modified vowel. A little added yawn sensation also helps a vowel find its necessary space. But, when an upper range word or phrase needs something extra, that's when vowel modifications come in.

When modifying, don't forget to "point" the voice mentally through the imaginary hole-in-the-wall. This will insure that vowels don't fall too far back in the throat - even those that are somewhat rounded anyway, such as OH or AH.

If you don't like what you hear on your first try, adjust the radio dial. Play with the feel of the IH as it combines with the original EE vowel sound until you feel the voice delicately "tune in" the tone. Remember, a little bit of "IH" goes a long way to modify the EE to a rounder, more comfortable tone. This goes for any instance when modifying vowels. Practice vowel modifications in songs, using the following basic guidelines.

VOWEL MODIFICATION GUIDELINES

✔   Locate the pure vowel of the syllable that's causing the trouble. (Don't modify the second part of any diphthong!)

✔   Find the pure vowel on the chart of vowel modifications.

✔   Look to the right on the chart to determine what modifier you should use.

✔   Sing the line, *imagining* the modifier vowel, while singing the pure vowel in question.

✔   If your tone needs a little something more, add a bit of yawn, support, or focus until the tone is full and round.

MUSICAL EXAMPLE
TURNING THEORY INTO PRACTICE

A good phrase to demonstrate vowel modifications comes from the memorable composition, "The Greatest Love of All" (words and music by Linda Creed and Michael Masser, © 1977, Gold Horizon Music Corp. and Golden Tropics Music Corp.). The second chorus contains an added top note near the end of the phrase "Can't take away my dignity."

On the word *my*, the singer may choose to insert a high E instead of the B written in the original music.

<Musical Excerpt #7>

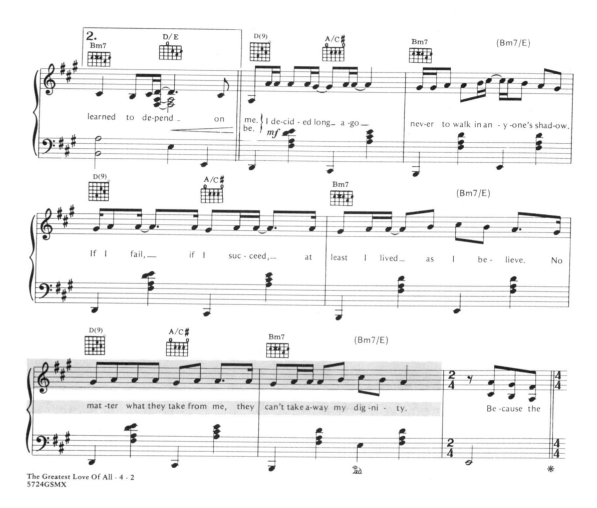

The Greatest Love Of All - 4 - 2
5724GSMX

<Musical Excerpt #8>

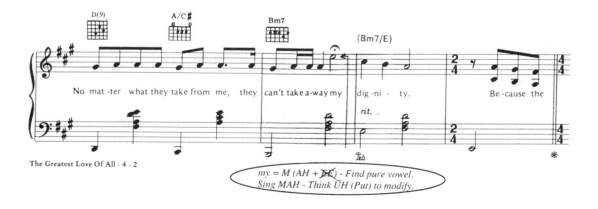

The Greatest Love Of All - 4 - 2

my = M (AH + EE) - Find pure vowel.
Sing MAH - Think ŪH (Put) to modify.

167

This particular type of note (at the top of a long interval or jump) gives singers a lot of trouble. If you darken the vowel, however, it's easy to reach the note without straining. Here's how to handle this particular situation:

First, notice that the vowel sound in the word "my" is a diphthong. Separate the sound into its composite vowels: AH and EE. When singing diphthongs, you sustain the *first* vowel primarily, dropping in the second vowel sound at the very last second (more on this later in Chapter 22: Compound Vowels).

With proper preparation, you can dramatically hold the word "my" with a full, rounded tone. Just be sure to carry out these necessary counterbalancing procedures:

- ✔ Take a low breath before the phrase
- ✔ Counterbalance
- ✔ Anchor the tone in the mouth
- ✔ Get into a good P.O.V.
- ✔ Think a little ŪH (put) into the sound

If your adjustment is correct, you'll hear the AH sound of "my" modify slightly toward AW (as in "saw"). If the tone still isn't full enough, you probably didn't clearly imagine the ŪH (put) sound while singing on AH. When done successfully, this will darken the vowel, freeing the throat, and rounding out the tone in general. Remember, you just need to *think* of the ŪH sound to create the vowel modification.

All this work goes into AH, the sustained portion of the diphthong. Just let the final constrictive EE fall into place as you sing through to the following word, "dignity."

Using songs in your repertoire, practice modifying the top notes in the upper range passages. Keep practicing until you find the right amount of darkening. In time (and with practice, of course), the vowel modifications will become second nature.

The next time you find yourself face-to-face with a "high" note, you'll find your knowledge of vowel modifications makes life in the "upper" range much easier.

CHAPTER 16
EXERCISE: THE GREAT SCALE

"The ultimate knowledge in vocal training is to transfer as much knowledge as possible from the conscious to the unconscious mind."

E. Herbert Caesari
The Alchemy of Voice

PUTTING IT TO THE TEST

The **Great Scale** has historically been one of the major tests of breath control, blend and anchoring. It also happens to offer one of the best opportunities to practice vowel modifications.

There's a dramatic difference between darkening and not darkening vowels when you sing in the upper range. Perhaps the best way to understand this is to *hear* it. Listen to the examples of the Great Scale at the end of the CD.

In the first example, the vowel is sung as purely as possible. Notice the brittle and yell-like result. Now listen to the second example, where the same vowel is sung, but this time it's darkened appropriately. Notice how the second example seems much easier, and has a full, rounded tone on top.

<EXERCISE #15: THE GREAT SCALE NOW IT'S YOUR TURN. . .>

Start the Great Scale on a pure AH. Allow the first run to sound yell-like, then seek out a rounder sound as you darken through the top of the second attempt, using the ŬH thought to relax the throat.

With some voices, it works better to modify certain vowels with an alternate vowel rather than the typical modification. Experiment using both the regular modifications and the alternates (see chart on page 171). Eventually, you'll find your own set of perfect vowel modifications.

The **alternate vowel modifications** (marked by asterisks) usually come into play in the upper middle voice while the typical modifications are normally employed in the uppermost range.

ALTERNATE VOWEL MODIFICATIONS

ORIGINAL VOWEL SOUND	ALTERNATE MODIFIER	MODIFIER
EE as in "meet"	No Alternate	IH (sit)
EH as in "bet"	No Alternate	
ĂH as in "cat"	EH*	
AY as in "day" (a diphthong, but commonly sung as pure)	EH*	
OO as in "moon"	OH*	ŬH (put)
OH as in "boat"	No Alternate	
AH as in "father"	AW*	
UH as in "love"	No Alternate	
AW as in "saw"	No Alternate	

If your efforts seem a little shaky at first, you might have to glue the modification and the original vowel together with a *little* extra support. As you sing towards the top of the double-octave scale, imagine the modification while singing the original vowel, and press *a bit* from the lower support muscles being careful to equalize breath pressure and control.

Don't let the scale get too top or bottom heavy. *Remember: when you move to higher notes, add space in the mouth and throat, by minutely darkening the vowels. When you sing low, add a little mask brilliance. In other words, when you sing up, think down; and when you sing down, think up.*

<MUSICAL EXAMPLE OF THE GREAT SCALE>

As you sing through the two octaves of this scale, both ascending and descending, elevate the voice mentally on the way down the scale too, as you support your tone carefully all the way through each repetition.

Exercise 15

Version 1: Ah
Version 2: Ee

CHAPTER 17

ENDURANCE EXERCISES: GROUP 2

"The object of art is expression. The essence of expression is imagination. The control of imagination is form. The medium of all three is technique."

Herbert Witherspoon

BUILDING VOCAL ENDURANCE: EXERCISE GROUP 2

Your instrument will grow stronger as you do the work outlined in these chapters. With stronger muscles, you can perform more demanding exercises and songs. But you must not content yourself only with that. On top of strength, you must also build agility, which gives you the flexibility to execute fast scale-like runs and jumps that appear in all styles of music.

You must stretch your voice to keep any stiffness from setting into the muscles. That's partly what these exercises are designed to do. They are well worth your time and effort. When free from stiffness, your muscles can respond to your inner directives. In other words, whatever you imagine, you will be able to sing!

ABOUT THESE EXERCISES

This group of exercises will take you higher and require you to sing faster. They will extend your breath longer than those in the previous group. In addition, they focus on dynamics. By dynamics, we mean a range of volume changes, from very loud to very soft. It is through well-developed dynamics that you can add interest and style to your performances.

These exercises may seem a bit demanding at first. But as you use your knowledge of the Secrets of Singing, they will quickly become easily manageable.

EXERCISE #16: THE DOUBLE ARPEGGIO

This exercise has two variations. You need to become familiar with both.

The first variation is similar to the double five-note exercise you worked on in the first endurance group. In the previous exercise, you hummed the first scale, then sang it again to one of the five basic vowels (HUM AH, HUM EE, etc.). This time, however, you'll sing AH (rather than hum) and then match one of the remaining four basic vowels to it. The objective is to develop the same open and anchored feeling on EE, EH, OO, OH, IH, etc. as comes naturally to AH.

In addition, you'll be singing through an even higher range. Remember to check your posture. Also, when you sing the EE, EH, OO, and OH, be sure you feel a roomy interior space behind and above the tongue - it should match what you feel when you sing the AH vowel. To achieve the match, let AH always take the lead.

In the second variation of this exercise, *you use only a single vowel sound for each pair,* as follows:

<Musical Example: Double Arpeggio on One Vowel>

This time, you'll be working on dynamics. Sing the first vowel sound, up and down the arpeggio medium loud. Then sing the second of each pair as softly as you can. Both times, however, sing both vowels with a full voice and with the tone well-anchored to firm up the feel of an open throat and focused release of tone.

EXERCISE #17 - TRIPLE-NOTE RUNS

Next, a velocity exercise to increase stamina, breath control and agility. In it, you sing 57 notes on one breath at a very fast pace. The pattern runs as follows:

✔ Sing three notes up
✔ Return to the first note of each triple note group
✔ Move a step up the scale
✔ Repeat the pattern

Written in music, it looks like this:

<Musical Example: Triple-Note Runs>

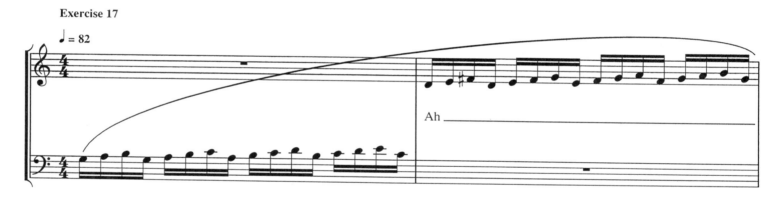

etc.

Listen carefully to the sample of this exercise on the accompanying CD. Notice how precisely the performer articulates each and every tone. You should articulate your notes in the same way.

Don't just slide through this exercise as though you were playing a slide whistle. The more you can sing each and every one of the 57 tones of each repetition, the better. Tap in each note by using a very active diaphragm and lower breathing system.

Keep those tones moving along the pathway, and keep the pressure from the breath support system light, but consistent. Use your "laughing" diaphragm as you did in the diaphragm exercise.

EXERCISE #18 - OCTAVE JUMPS

Octave jumps are an excellent rehearsal for the wide-ranging leaps from note to note so often found in opera, as well as in rock and jazz vocal compositions. In this exercise, you leap an octave (that is, thirteen consecutive black and white keys on the piano above the first tone), while keeping the volume level equal between the upper and lower tones.

Be sure to keep your jaw in the same position for the top and bottom tones. Don't sock the top note of each pair just because it's higher. Make the whole series of notes equal in volume. Don't let your jaw become rigid as you negotiate the intervals. Alternate vowels or select one in particular that needs extra work.

<Musical Example: Octave Jumps>

(H)AH AH AH AH AH AH AH

EXERCISE #19: MID-RANGE INVENTORY: INITIATE A TONE, TURN UP TO A SIX-COUNT MESSA di VOCE, THEN DOWN A SCALE.

It's always necessary to regularly check the way tones are started. In this exercise, *gently* take a breath, then *gently* initiate a tone in the upper-middle range. Make a turn and then hold the top note.

On the top note, during a quick count of six, let the note swell louder and then return to a medium volume. Finally, sing down the scale to an octave below. Another "inventory" exercise, this drill brings many techniques together, balancing and working at the crucial upper middle section of your range.

<Musical Example: Mid-Range Inventory>

Exercise 19

Version 1: Ah _____

etc.

EXERCISE #20: BROKEN 1, 4, 5 CHORDS

Many songs from all types of vocal music are based on the chords built on the tonic, sub-dominant and dominant chords of the major scale. In other words, these are note combinations spelled out by using a formula for constructing major chords built on the first, fourth and fifth tones of a major or common scale. By walking (vocally) through these chords and linking them up in one un-broken line we arrive at a great exercise for sustaining long lines of tone, counterbalancing, and P.O.V.

<Musical Example: 1, 4, 5 Exercise>

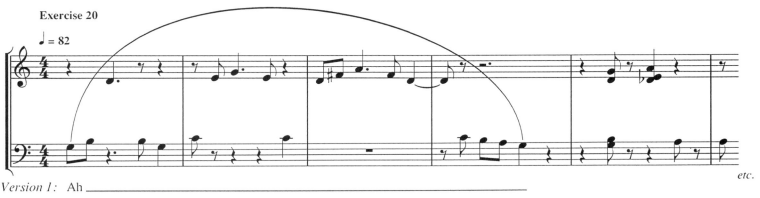

Version 1: Ah _____
Version 2: Ee _____

Listen to the demonstration of this exercise on your CD. Use one breath for each group of notes that make up the three broken chords. Now you try it: As you get to the top of the higher repetitions, use vowel modifications to keep your tone under control.

PART THREE
A FREE VOICE: THE POWER OF AN OPEN THROAT

CHAPTER 18

SIMULTANEITY

"The ideal tone, is a mouthful of sound that 'spins', remoulds itself for every vowel, is felt at the lips, in the head, presses down the tongue, pushes up the...{roof of the mouth}, even descends into the chest, in fact fills every nook and cranny."

Giovanni Battista Lamperti

PUTTING IT ALL TOGETHER: BUILDING YOUR BEST VOICE

Vocal ease throughout your range requires not only the perfect application of everything discussed up to this point, but *timely* coordination of these techniques as well. The best word to describe the event that must take place to allow freedom of vocal production at any point in a singer's range is **simultaneity**. Now, not only must you know what the component parts of great singing are, but they must be *executed all together at exactly the same time.*

GETTING OUT OF YOUR OWN WAY

Simultaneity is achieved by delegating much of the technical side of the work to your subconscious. That's why you've been steadfastly practicing the exercises while reading this book; practice puts the concepts deep into the memory of your bones and muscles.

COORDINATION

Bringing together the many aspects of singing is at the same time the greatest challenge and the most rewarding aspect of learning a powerful vocal technique. A singer is required in the end to coordinate many muscular movements, some above the voice box and some below. No one concept or technique is the end all in singing know-how. Focus will not make you a singer. Anchoring, mouth position, blend, counterbalancing, etc. are only of value when used collectively. Singing requires that each new technique is placed (better yet) practiced into the unconscious mind. It has to be so before words and emotions come to life. The Italians say they take technique on stage with them stored in their little finger.

Muscles within our voluntary control need to be managed delicately. Conscious muscular effort is of value only as long as it doesn't interfere with the natural workings of your innate talent. In other words, whatever learned skills you inherit from a book or lessons will be useful as long as they don't interfere with whatever natural abilities you started with.

Successful coordination of willpower and technique gives a singer the capacity to convey to others the feeling and ideas of songs. In the end, you must exercise your will not only upon one part of the vocal instrument, but on the *integration* of all parts of the instrument.

Some singers are great breathers. Some excel in focus or blending vocal colors. There are many vocalists who have exceptional ring in their voices. But the singer who consistently steals the show on stages, in clubs, and on recordings everywhere, *is the one who has put it all together and sings beautifully.*

ILLUSTRATION #18.1 - Simultaneity

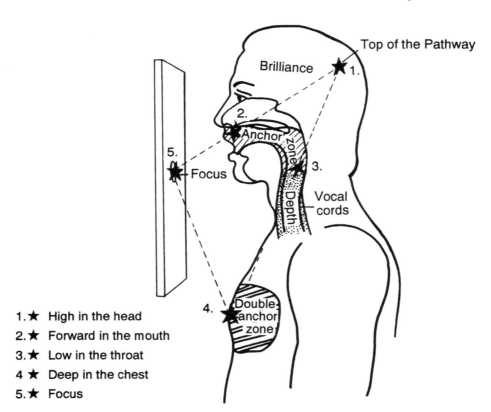

1.★ High in the head
2.★ Forward in the mouth
3.★ Low in the throat
4 ★ Deep in the chest
5.★ Focus

TIMING IS EVERYTHING

Timing cements all the preceding information of this book into place. When effective breathing, focus, anchoring and blend habits are in place and working together, the result can only be in tones that partake of all the secrets of singing at once.

The singing process must go far beyond "I take a good breath now <u>and then</u> open my mouth <u>and then</u>...etc." *Everything has to happen simultaneously.* Your must bring everything you know about singing to each and every sung tone.

CONCLUSION: THE HALLMARK OF A FREE VOICE: THE OPEN THROAT

The result of adding together simultaneously all this technical wisdom is nothing less than the most sought after quality of all - the *OPEN THROAT.*

There are many traits that indicate whether or not your throat is open and relaxed. The most obvious is that singing, in any part of your range, feels easy and natural.

The open throat allows vibration to move to all resonators, at once giving the tone a clear, ringing quality. You'll notice that you can sing through your entire range without cracking or unwanted deviations of tone quality.

EXERCISE #21: TWO FIVE-NOTE SCALES, A TWO-OCTAVE JUMP, HOLD FOR THREE BEATS, TURN, THEN DOWN A SCALE

In preparation for this type of "holistic" singing where the emphasis is on doing everything at once rather than thinking of one concept or another as you vocalize, sing two ascending and then descending five-note scales.

After the last note on the way down the second scale, launch into the following note which is a full two octaves above the last note of the scale and hold it for three beats, then turn the voice around to sing down the scale.

As you sing the scale notes (the penultimates) just before leaping to the top tone, that's the time to focus, shape the mouth or otherwise "fix" the instrument for the upcoming top note. Be sure to bear down adequately with the diaphragm against the support muscles. This insures the top notes aren't overblown as they come into full bloom during the three count hold. After that, it must be a "leap of faith" that it'll be there.

And that's just what singing must be for you now. Faith that your technique will get you vocally to whatever musical or emotional destination you have in mind.

Practice this exercise on all vowels until you can pre-set the sound of the upcoming top note in the two short scales preceding it. How you handle the breath, focus, pathway, blend, etc. are part of a complete response to your willing the note to sound as you conceive it in mind before ever giving out the sound. *Hearing a top note a split second before singing it coordinates its technical parts into a well-tuned whole sound.*

**<Musical Example: Two Five-Note Scales,
A Two-Octave Jump, Hold for Three Beats,
Turn, then down a Scale>**

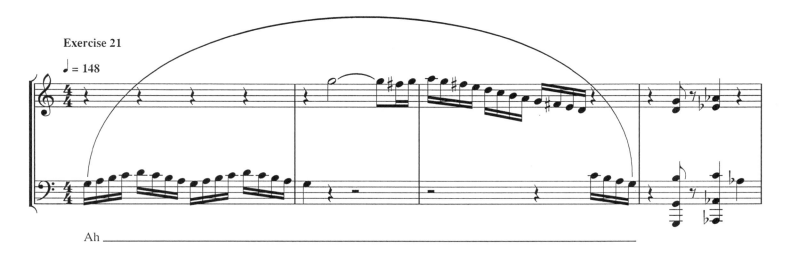

Exercise 21

♩ = 148

Ah _____

CHAPTER 19

VIBRATO

"It is not only by yielding to one's impulses that one achieves greatness, but also by patiently filing away the steel wall that separates what one feels from what one is capable of doing."

Vincent Van Gogh

VOCAL MOVEMENT

Along with an open throat, a regular **vibrato** is the best indicator that the voice is truly free and open. When an unshakably straight or wobbly vocal tone finally yields and settles into a supple, yet restrained movement, known as vibrato, the instrument has truly been elevated in stature.

Vibrato is a natural attribute of the human instrument; it isn't *added* to the voice, but *unveiled* as poor singing habits are dissolved through correct practice. A subtle, even vibrato brings vibrance and warmth to your voice.

Basically, vibrato is a fluctuation of pitch and intensity. It's the quality of the human voice that guitarists (among other string players) try to duplicate with a rigorous motion of the left hand on the guitar neck.

In a good vibrato, the voice fluctuates anywhere from a quarter-tone (half the distance between two neighboring keys on the piano) to almost a full step (two neighboring keys) above and below the pitch you're singing. Vibrato also may fluctuate ever so slightly with changes in pitch or intensity. As the pitch or intensity rises, the rate of vocal movement sometimes increases; as the pitch falls, the intensity may decrease.

HOW VIBRATO IS PRODUCED

Characteristic of the inner workings of the vocal mechanism are delicate nerve impulses transmitted to the muscles of the larynx. This rhythmic, recurring supply of nerve energy causes the fluctuation of tone known as vibrato. The outcome of this regular sequence of nerve impulses allows the cords to resist the flow of air moving up the windpipe.

As the vocal muscles alternately energize and then relax, the tone reflects these changes by sounding in minute peaks and valleys. (One cycle of vibrato = one peak + one trough. See Illustration #19.1)

ILLUSTRATION #19.1 - Cycles of Vibrato

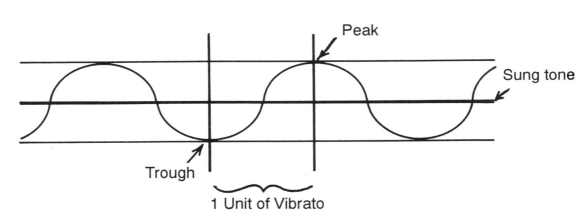

THE FREQUENCY OF A PLEASING VIBRATO

Vocal specialists have carefully evaluated the vibrato of dozens of top-notch professional singers. In studying these voices, they discovered that these singers' vibrato consistently averaged somewhere between 6 and 7 cycles per second (meaning the cords bow up and down six to seven times per second). This is called the *frequency* of the vibrato.

While it's good to know this information, don't worry too much about whether the frequency of your vibrato is 5.9999 or 6.3259 cycles per second. If something's wrong with your vibrato, you'll know it; impaired **vocal movement** (another term describing vibrato, or vibrato-like conditions) is usually a lot, not a little, off the mark. A troubled vibrato is usually completely absent, way too slow, or way too fast.

USE YOUR INTUITION

Vibrato is similar to the idle of a car. When it's functioning properly, you feel the idling, but you're accustomed to it, and you really don't give it much thought. It's kind of a steady, pleasing purr. When it's not idling too fast or too slow, the assumption is that the engine is doing fine and there's nothing to worry about.

But if the idle is too slow or too fast, you're aware of it every time you stop at a red light. One begins to worry about the engine, because the idle is an indication of a car's overall condition.

It's the same with the voice. If your instrument produces a vibrato, and it sounds okay to you (and those who listen to you), it's probably just fine.

IRREGULAR VOCAL MOVEMENT

Many singers have vocal movement that doesn't conform to the norm. Sometimes this becomes an unacceptable trademark. Correcting vocal movement that's irritating can enhance the vocalist's overall image. Tone with no vibrato is called a **straight tone**, a vibrato that's too slow is called a **wobble**, and a vibrato that's too fast is known as a **tremolo** (see Illustration #19.2 below).

ILLUSTRATION #19.2 - Vibrato, Wobble, and Tremolo

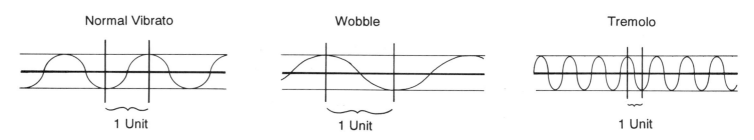

Normal Vibrato	Wobble	Tremolo
1 Unit	1 Unit	1 Unit

How can you tell if you have any of these problems? Tape yourself singing a song, or just holding a note on a vowel. Timing the frequency (the number of peaks and valleys per second) and using your own intuition is the best judge of the quality of your vibrato. If your voice's vocal movement strays seriously away from six to seven beats a second or is straight with no motion at all, now is as good a time as any to work for a more pleasing vibrato.

A Straight Tone

Singers often complain that there isn't any vibrato in their voice at all. Straight tone is usually caused by tension in the throat, weak breath control/support systems, or a combination of both. To correct a straight tone, work on relaxing the throat, neck and shoulders, while strengthening the breath muscles using the two exercises described CHAPTER 2.

A Wobble or Tremolo? Catch Up on Your Breath Work!

Wobbling occurs when the frequency of the vibrato is substantially slower than 6 to 7 cycles per second (usually somewhere in the area of 3 to 5 cycles per second).

There are some pop, rock 'n roll, and musical theatre singers who use the wobble as a vocal effect, but on the whole, an audience quickly tires of this sound. Wobbling is usually caused by insufficient breath support to the cords.

On the other hand, tremolo occurs when the frequency of the vibrato is higher than 7.0 cycles per second (in the range of 9.0 to 10.0 cycles per second). If you sing regularly with tremolo, instead of a healthy vibrato, you're probably putting more of a strain on your audience than on your voice.

With a tremolo, the speed of the fluctuations tends to irritate and create nervousness in the listener. Obviously, that's the last thing an audience wants to feel when they've come to be entertained. Tremolo is usually caused by exerting too much pressure on the cords from the lower breath support muscles, or just tremendous nervous agitation on the part of the singer.

THE GOOD NEWS ABOUT VIBRATO

There's no one exercise that will "give" you a perfect vibrato. If you have no vibrato at all, a wobble or a tremolo, it's an indication that you need to do more work on the basics.

The good news is that a smooth, even vibrato appears as if by magic when the secrets of singing are mastered and well-integrated. It's an indication that your throat is open and relaxed, and the cords are vibrating freely.

The correct application of support, focus, anchoring, blend, etc., is a prerequisite for a healthy vibrato. All of the characteristics of effective technique must work together to allow the cords to operate normally. When the strength of the cords and the airflow from the lower breath support muscles are well balanced, vibrato will most likely take care of itself.

HAVE PATIENCE WHILE YOU PRACTICE

You'll need to have patience. Practicing to encourage a smooth, even vibrato is like starting a gas-powered lawn mower. If all of the conditions are right, and you pull the starter cord enough times, the engine will eventually turn over and the mower will run smoothly.

The same will happen to your vibrato if you persevere in practicing the vocal work outlined in these pages.

A PROGRESS REPORT

Because vibrato depends on the integration of all of the fundamental techniques, it can be used as one of the indicators of your vocal progress. In essence, *vibrato is one of the gifts your voice gives back to you for taking good care of it.* The following exercises will create the conditions in the voice which allow a healthy vibrato to show itself.

EXERCISE #22: HALF-STEP TRILLING

One of the best exercises you can do to encourage a pleasing vibrato is to sing a note and its half-step neighbor, (one black or white key away, up or down, on a keyboard). A half-step is a convenient jumping-off point in your efforts to establish a controlled vibrato.

First sing the original note, then its half-step neighbor, then back to the original note, alternating back and forth between the two notes. In each repetition, there's a slow increase in the speed of the switching from note to note.

Make the peaks and valleys as even as possible. As you become proficient at this exercise you may want to practice the same exercise with the notes just slightly sharp (about 1/4 step higher than the beginning note), then becoming just slightly flat, again, about 1/4 step below the note. (A 1/4 step is half as much distance between each note as heard between two neighboring tones on the piano.) Written in music, this exercise looks something like this:

<Musical Example:
Half-Step Trilling Vibrato Exercise>

Bend the tone slightly up and down, up and down, slowly increasing the speed until you can't control it anymore. Listen to the example on the CD and repeat. If you lose control, stop; then repeat the exercise.

As your coordination increases, you'll be able to keep the vibrating motion even and controlled. If the musical example on the tape is too fast for you, memorize it and then practice it at your own pace (or if you have a tape recorder that has an adjustable speed feature, you can set the speed to a comfortable level and slowly increase the speed as your coordination increases). Join the CD when you've increased your speed and can follow along comfortably.

EXERCISE #23: ASCENDING SCALE, DESCENDING SCALE - EACH NOTE WITH EIGHT BEATS

Another good exercise for vibrato preparation (and maintenance, if you already have a pleasing vibrato) is the eight-beat, eight-note exercise.

<Musical Example: Ascending Scale, Descending Scale - Each Note with Eight Beats>

Version 1: AH _____
Version 2: EE _____

Listen carefully to the example on the accompanying CD, then try it yourself. Sing up a scale and then slowly descend back through the same notes. On the way down, give each note eight *gentle* pulses, all controlled by the down and out countermotion of the diaphragm and ribs. When breath is balanced you'll feel as if the tone is flowing backwards through the reversed megaphone.

Add A Little Bounce, And You've Got It

The diaphragm and lower support muscles will feel as if they're gently bouncing as you pulse the voice eight times on each pitch down the scale. In fact, the feeling in your abdomen is somewhat less, but similar to what you feel when you have a good "belly-laugh." It's a good idea to laugh for five or ten seconds (just fake it, if you have to) to get an indication of what this exercise should feel like in and around the lower support muscles.

If you're having a little trouble staying with the examples on the CD, here's a little hint to make the exercise easier (while still maintaining its effectiveness): *emphasize the first and the fifth notes.* This will give the exercise more structure and help keep you on track (see Musical Example above).

These two exercises, like the Messa di Voce exercise, are long term work and will improve over time. Again, be patient with your vibrato. Have faith that if you follow the basics described in this book, your vibrato will reveal itself when all of the elements of singing become integrated.

CHAPTER 20

ADVANCED EXERCISES:
ENDURANCE GROUP 3

*"Practice means to perform, over and over again in the face of
all obstacles, some act of vision, of faith, of desire. Practice is a means
of inviting the perfection desired."*

Martha Graham

FOCUS ON QUALITY, NOT QUANTITY

Hour after hour of practice is not necessarily the best thing you can do for your voice. It's not how long you practice, it's how well you do it. Engage in practice thoughtfully. You are involved in an investigation of your hidden vocal powers.

A vocal workout offers the perfect time to check out your vocal accomplishments, and to discover new resources you've never tapped before. Hours of singing up and down the scale without purposefully trying to achieve a better sense of pathway, focus, and P.O.V. aren't even worth your time or trouble.

PRACTICING ISN'T PAINLESS, BUT IT IS THE PATH TO YOUR DREAMS

Working with the systematic regimen of exercises gathered in these pages will allow you to develop invaluable singing skills. You'll build power into your voice, achieve range extension, breath control and support, volume control and flexibility. But you won't see this happen simply by reading these pages. You've got to carry out the repetitions of the exercises themselves. Also, your practice has to be consistent.

Day-by-day progress is faster at first. Then it slows down as you become more accomplished. After awhile, day-by-day improvement may seem microscopic, at best. You'll also reach plateaus, stages where you seem to be working forever to reach the next level. Don't get discouraged. Consistent work *will* get you there.

EXAMPLE #24: VARIABLE VOWEL EXERCISE

In this one, take our by now familiar arpeggio up on an AH vowel to its top note and then repeat that note four times as you sing through the other four basic vowels. The exercise looks like this:

<Musical Example: Variable Vowel Exercise>

Give a listen to the demonstration of the exercise on the CD. Be sure not to move your mouth too much as you pass through the five vowels. As you sing higher and higher into your range, you'll be surprised how little mouth movement it takes to emit all five vowels. The best order for the vowels in this exercise is AH, EE, EH, OO, and OH. Sing AH first since it naturally opens up the throat and mouth. Make sure each vowel pathway leads through the reversed megaphone to the hole-in-the-wall.

Counterbalance, modify the vowels, if necessary, and keep the feel of all vowels anchored in the mouth. The inner lining of the mouth - sides, roof, surface of the tongue, and back wall, should feel alive with vibration when you're well anchored. Remember, tones that are truly free and floating are not put or placed too emphatically anywhere but are allowed to flow along the pathway through the instrument, finding resonance everywhere.

EXERCISE #25: NINE-NOTE SCALE
MERGING VOWELS WHILE ASCENDING

This is a special exercise for line, blend and overall consistency of tone. Sing the same nine note scale used in Exercise Group 2. As you go up the scale, actually change the vowel from what you started with to the next vowel in the list below. In other words, as you sing up the scale on EE, as you get 3 or 4 notes from the top, glide into an EH sound; then sing back down the scale on EH. The pattern is as follows:

NINE-NOTE SCALE
(Merging Vowels)

START ON:	CHANGE ON THE WAY UP TO:
EE	EH
EH	OO
OO	OH
OH	AH
AH	EE

Listen to the sample and repeat to be sure you understand the way it goes.

<Musical Example: Nine-Scale Merging Vowels>

Exercise 25

Version 1: EE _____ eh

Try this exercise with the secondary vowels listed at the end of Endurance Group 1. Use any mixture of sounds you want. The most beneficial work is accomplished when merging vowels which cause the mouth to somewhat close, with vowels that are sung with the mouth wide open and vice-versa; such as EE to AH, OO to EH, or OH to EE.

EXERCISE #26 - TWO-OCTAVE ARPEGGIO

So you say you want something a little more challenging. Alright. Give this one a try. It's just like the single arpeggios you practice already. The difference is this exercise goes twice as high and twice as fast. The result is you have to rely more on your instincts and subconscious rather than thinking your way through the sung tones.

There's just not time to think very much so relying on your good habits is the order of the day. Just let loose and blow through the arpeggios allowing the Secrets of Singing to pave the way. Listen to the musical sample and then go for it. Be sure to keep plenty of space between your upper and lower molars to insure the back of your throat stays open.

<Musical Example: Two-Octave Arpeggio>

EXERCISE #27: REVERSE TWO-OCTAVE ARPEGGIO

A quick check of your initiation is in order here. Let's now take the same exercise and reverse it so you start at the top, work your way down and then skip back up to the top, and even hold for the count of three once you get all the way up. It looks like this on paper:

<Musical Example: Reverse Two-Octave Arpeggio
with Hold on Top>

Now listen to the CD of your choice. As you're starting from the upper part of your range and working your way down, the first note and especially the last note will have to be well modified. The top note at the end of each repetition can be especially thorny because you've exhausted a good part of your air by the time you have to hold for three counts. Counterbalance by keeping your focus low, breath support steadied with diaphragmatic resist and add some chest resonance for good measure. In the upper range, the feel of breath support pressing against the back of your sternum (breast-bone) indicates the tone's blend is well adjusted. A little bit of the yawn sensation throughout the exercise will ensure that your throat stays open.

EXERCISE #28: VARIABLE VOWELS, THREE-OCTAVE JUMPS

As in the second exercise of this group, take the basic vowels in this order: EE, EH, OO, OH, AH and sing them together on a low note, jump an octave to a middle note of the same name and then jump up an octave again to the note two octaves above the original tone.

Each jump will require you to rely on all of your technique simultaneously. Be sure to aim for the center of each tone and try to imagine (hear!) the tone quality, pitch and intensity level you would like to have before singing each tone. The more clearly you can hear the tones before you sing them the better they'll sound as you give them out.

<Musical Example: Variable Vowels, Three-Octave Jumps>

Exercise 28

♩ = 148

ee eh oo oh ah   *etc.*

ee oh oo oh ah

etc.

PART FOUR:

PHRASING – THE MARK OF THE PROFESSIONAL

CHAPTER 21

THE ELEMENTS OF PHRASING

"The thing that influenced me most was the way Tommy [Dorsey] played his trombone. . . It was my idea to make my voice work in the same way as a trombone or violin - not sounding like them, but 'playing' the voice like those instrumentalists."

Frank Sinatra

THE SIGNIFICANCE OF CONNECTING TONES SMOOTHLY

The way you connect tones can make or break your singing. No matter how much breath control and support you have; no matter how focused your voice is, your audience isn't going to be interested for very long if your lines don't flow.

For example, if I . . . . . . wrote like. . . . . this. . . . . .how . . . . long would. . . . . .you. . . .stay interested in . . . . what I. . . . . . . .was . . . . . .saying? In all forms of artistic communication, whether it be poetry, a movie, a painting, or singing, how effectively the artist connects thoughts together in the chosen medium is one of the key elements of the work.

In songs, the flow of ideas and words is intricately linked with meaning and your ability to convey the emotional content of songs.

CREATING YOUR OWN VOCAL SIGNATURE

By connecting notes together, you insure that each note has the characteristics of your best sound. Consistency is what will build your style. The reason that singers like Frank Sinatra, Luciano Pavarotti, Ray Charles, Paul McCartney, Barbra Streisand, or Aretha Franklin have such instantly recognizable voices is that they always sing consistently.

After a few seconds of listening to any of these vocalists, their own unique way of joining notes together becomes obvious. Along with the tonal quality of their voice, what makes them instantly recognizable is their phrasing.

When you hear singers on commercials who are paid to imitate the voices of singing stars, you hear them imitating the stars' phrasing. This is very much like comedians who do imitations of celebrities. They imitate the voice, of course, but they also imitate the gestures. That's what really makes an impression successful.

For singers, phrasing is a specific kind of gesture that creates your own vocal signature. Needless to say, any time spent on practicing phrasing is time well spent.

PHRASING BEGINS WITH THE BASICS

It's impossible to achieve smooth, connected lines without first having laid the groundwork. More than any other technique discussed in this book, the foundation of flowing line lies in the synthesis of the basics.

As one begins to initiate rather than attack phrases, develop good breath control and support, learns how to focus, anchor, handle vowels and blend tones simultaneously, the study of phrasing becomes feasible.

CREATING "SINGERLY" LINES

Good phrasing is one of the essential elements of professional singing. In a nutshell, it's what makes a voice sound singerly (you won't find this word in any dictionary - it's the author's own concoction).

The ability to create good phrases is the vocal equivalent to using effective sentence structure in speech.

There are many terms that are associated with, or synonymous with phrasing: line, connecting, sostenuto (Italian for "sustaining"), and legato (another Italian word meaning "to bind or tie") are just a few. All of these terms refer to a smooth, flowing tone which is uninterrupted by sudden volume changes, unsteady breath support, overbearing consonants, or misplaced breaths.

Unfortunately, phrasing is one of the most underrated aspects of singing. However, performers have been aware of the importance of phrasing for a long time.

William Shakespeare, the great English playwright, through the voice of Hamlet, warned actors to "Speak the speech trippingly on the tongue. But if you mouth it, as many of our players do, I had as lief the town crier spoke my lines."

Hamlet was written approximately 400 years ago. It's obvious that serious stage performers have studied for centuries, ways to improve the flow of words in speech and song.

THE ELEMENTS OF GOOD PHRASING

To thoroughly study the nuances of phrasing, here's a list of the most important components to consider:

- ✔ Compound Vowels
- ✔ Singing on Vowels Only
- ✔ Maintaining Intensity
- ✔ Breathing for Phrasing
- ✔ Consonants

As with all aspects of singing covered so far, it takes time, patience, and most of all, practice, to achieve a smooth, flowing tone. However, just as a business person's success is dependent to a large degree on their command of the language (i.e., on how they construct sentences), your phrasing will be one of the factors that determines whether you sing in the shower or in the great concert venues around the world.

CHAPTER 22
COMPOUND VOWELS

"...tone is nothing but vowelized breath."

McLennan

NOT ALL VOWELS ARE CREATED EQUAL

Though diphthongs were introduced earlier in Chapter 8, a more detailed examination is in order. When practicing phrasing, it's important to build the habit of singing one vowel at a time. It sounds easy enough, but you may not be aware that vowel sounds are formed in various ways.

In the practice exercises, you've been using pure vowels; however, when singing songs, you also encounter *compound vowels*. Compound vowels are two or three vowel sounds sung or spoken in rapid succession. (When a vowel sound is created from two pure vowels, it's called a **diphthong**; when it's created from three pure vowels, it's called a **triphthong**.)

Compound vowels require careful consideration. They can obstruct the pathway by causing extra movement of the mouth parts that can disrupt the flow of phrases.

WHAT ARE THE COMPOUND VOWELS?

The compound vowel chart below shows the most common diphthongs and their components. This will help you know what to look for when you're practicing songs. In the column on the right, the capitalized and bolded sound is the sung or sustained portion of the syllable. The sounds indicated by the lower case letters are the delayed part of the diphthong. (The second portion of any compound vowel is delayed to prevent it from prematurely obstructing the open or pure initial vowel just preceding it.)

Notice that each of these diphthongs ends on an OO or EE. That's the trouble with giving both parts of a compound vowel equal emphasis. The OO or EE portion closes the throat, compared to the first part of the diphthong. So, use the first or "singing" part of the compound vowel to sustain the tone and end with the delayed or trailing portion of the compound vowel.

Some vocal styles (country music is a good example) feature the second half of the diphthong. There's nothing wrong with this practice, as long as the constrictive OO and EE vowels have been worked out so that they don't pinch the tone and cause the singer undue strain.

THIS DIPHTHONG	...SOUNDS LIKE...	AND IS MADE UP OF:
OW	Brown	ĂH + oo
AY	Day	EH + ee
OU	House	ĂH + oo
OH	Blow	UH + oo
EW	Few	EE + oo
I	Right	AH + ee

HOW TO SING COMPOUND VOWELS

Professional singers handle compound vowels in much the same way that they handle consonants. To minimize the disturbance of the line, sustain the first vowel sound as long as possible, before gently tapping in the delayed portion. Sometimes the delayed vowel is attached to the beginning of the next word to insure that it doesn't interfere with the line.

<Musical Example #9>

| | (a) Written | (b) Incorrectly sung | (c) Correctly sung |

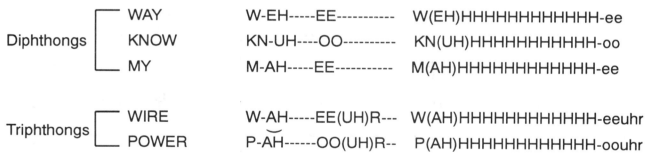

Diphthongs	WAY	W-EH-----EE-----------	W(EH)HHHHHHHHHHHHH-ee
	KNOW	KN-UH----OO----------	KN(UH)HHHHHHHHHHH-oo
	MY	M-AH-----EE-----------	M(AH)HHHHHHHHHHHH-ee
Triphthongs	WIRE	W-AH-----EE(UH)R---	W(AH)HHHHHHHHHHHHH-eeuhr
	POWER	P-AH------OO(UH)R--	P(AH)HHHHHHHHHHHH-oouhr

In these examples, notice how the first vowel sound is sustained for as long as possible, delaying the second (or third) portion of the compound vowel until the very last instant. Then it is dropped into the word *very gently*, just as if you were singing a non-obtrusive, minute final consonant.

SINGING TRIPHTHONGS

Triphthongs usually occur when a double vowel is followed by the consonant R, as in the following examples:

THIS TRIPHTHONG	SOUNDS LIKE . . .	AND IS MADE UP OF:
IR	Wire	**AH** + EE + uh
OUR/OWR	Devour/Power	**ÃH** + OO + uh

EXERCISE #29: NINE-NOTE SCALE - SPLITTING COMPOUND VOWELS

To be sure the concept of splitting diphthongs into two parts, singing and delayed, is felt instrumentally as well as understood, practice handling compound vowels correctly, as follows:

Take the nine-note scale used in Endurance Group One and sing up and down the scale on each of the six diphthongs, as listed on the Compound Vowel Chart. Be sure to hold off on the delayed part of the diphthong (see musical example) until the last note of the scale.

<Musical Example: Nine-Note Scale - Splitting Compound Vowels>

Exercise 29

Version 1: AH _____ oo

CHAPTER 23

EXERCISE: SINGING ON VOWELS ONLY

"One of the most important things for the student to know is that each vowel sound has its own individual quality. Nothing is so dull as a voice which has neutralized all vowels into one consistently bright or dark color..."

Ivan Trusler
Walter Ehret
Functional Lessons in Singing

A STRING OF PURE VOWELS

The following exercise will be tremendously helpful in learning how to create smooth, flowing lines. Beginners and professionals alike would do well to practice this exercise every time they learn a song.

The exercise is simple. Just delete all the consonants from a song, and sing the phrases on the remaining vowels. When you encounter diphthongs or triphthongs, break them down and sing them in their pure vowel sounds. Sustain the first vowel sound, dropping the second or third vowel into place at the very last moment.

For example, an excerpt from the song "From A Distance" (lyrics and music by Julie Gold, © 1987, Wing and Wheel Music and Julie Gold Music, B.M.I)., would look like this:

<Musical Example #10 (audio sample found at the end of the CD)>

From	a	distance,	the	world	looks
(Fr) **UH** (m)	**UH**	(d) **IH** (st) **UH** (ns)	(th) **UH** (w)	**UH** (rld)	(l) **ŬH** (ks)

blue	and	green	and	the	snow-	capped
(bl) **OO** **ĂH** (nd)	(gr) **EE** (n),	**ĂH** (nd)	(th) **UH**	(sn) **UH** oo	(c) **ĂH** (pt)	

mountains	white
(m) **ĂH** oo (nt) **EH** (ns)	(wh) **AH** ee (t)

If you know the tune, try singing the example above, singing only the capitalized vowel sounds. Make sure you sing the vowels the way they *sound*, and not the way they *look*. Take the word "mountain" as an example. Since it is written with two double vowels (m)**OU**(nt)**AI**(ns), it *looks* like it would be pronounced (m)**OH**-oo(nt)**AY**-ee(ns), but it actually sounds like (m)**AH**-oo(nt)**EH**(ns) Listen to the example at the end of your CD first to make sure you understand the exercise.

Also, be careful when practicing this exercise - certain consonants (such as l, w, n and r) have a tendency to stick to the vowels. *Make sure that you're singing only on vowels.*

Now take a song that you've memorized and write it out exactly like the example, then sing on the pure vowel sounds. It'll feel and sound a little strange at first, but after you practice a bit, you'll be amazed at how much this exercise helps to create beautiful, flowing phrases and really gets you vowel-oriented. Try it slowly at first, then build up to the original tempo.

Practicing this exercise on several songs you know will make you keenly aware of the string of tone on which the pearls of words are strung. You'll hear the underlying structure upon which the song is built. All that's left is to gently drop in the consonants.

After performing this exercise on several songs, you'll find that the way you approach songs will be entirely different. As vowels become more and more pure and emphasized, your singing will automatically improve. In a word, your sound will become more **professional**.

CHAPTER 24
MAINTAINING INTENSITY

"Personality... is the prime requisite of a great artist, with second and third places going to intelligence and hard work."

Weldon Whitlock

BE CONSISTENT!

Another important consideration in achieving singerly phrasing is to maintain consistent intensity. Intensity, in singing terms, is the amount of air that hits the cords at any one time.

Good breath support and control are necessary elements of maintaining consistent intensity. If you feel a little weak in these areas, make sure you're practicing your breath and Messa di Voce exercises regularly.

When you're in control of how much air hits the cords, you have amazing freedom; the entire vocal mechanism relaxes, and your sound naturally improves. Singers who have developed this control appear to sing effortlessly.

CHANGING VOLUME WHILE MAINTAINING CONSISTENT INTENSITY

Anytime intensity drops, there's the risk of losing tone quality and carrying power. Therefore, an increase in volume requires a moderated increase in intensity. A decrease in volume must occur without any sudden decrease in intensity.

How do you achieve this? Again, solid breath control and support are necessary. You must build these two elements until each note-to-note transition in a song, regardless of the pitches involved, is instantaneous, without any sudden shifts in power.

The next two exercises are designed to develop your ability to sing through a wide range of notes smoothly and with consistent intensity.

THE SEE-SAW EXERCISES

The see-saw exercises will provide you with the opportunity to practice singing smoothly through a wide range of intervals. An interval describes the distance between any two notes.

For most people, singing intervals that are small, meaning that there is not much distance between the two notes, is relatively easy. As the interval increases, however, it becomes increasingly difficult to maintain consistent intensity.

How many times have you heard inexperienced singers reach for an upper note by blasting the note with intensity? Even if the singer is able to hit the correct pitch, the vocal quality sounds wrong. This occurs when breath support or intensity is suddenly increased way out of proportion for what is actually required for the tone.

When the intensity of breath support and control is equalized, each note will be in tune and smoothly connected to the notes before and after it. Strive for this balance in the following exercises.

EXERCISE #30: SEE-SAW - ASCENDING

Both versions of the see-saw exercise are really just modified scales. In the ascending version, start with the key-note of a scale that is in your vocal range. (The key-note is the one you'll keep singing back to as you move through the intervals.) Now, from that note, sing up to the second note of the scale, then back to the key-note. Next, sing from the key-note to the third note of the scale, and back to the key-note. Then, key-note to the fourth note and back, etc., see-sawing your way up the scale.

<Musical Example: See-Saw Exercise - Ascending>

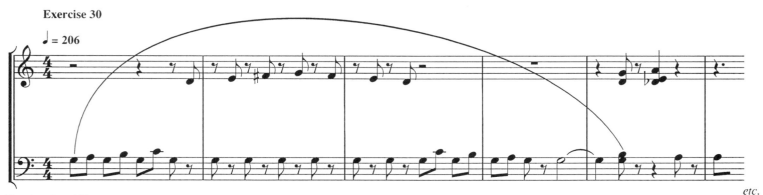

Version 1: AH _____   *etc.*

EXERCISE #31: SEE-SAW - DESCENDING

According to the laws of nature, what goes up must come down. The descending version of the see-saw puts the key-note on top. Starting at the top, sing down one step of the scale, then back up to the top. Next, sing down two notes and back up to the key-note. Continue until you reach an octave below the uppermost note; then climb back up note by note until you're back where you started. Be sure all tones are sung at the same moderate volume. Don't let the distance between tones, either on the way up or down force you to sing suddenly very soft or very loud.

<Musical Example:
See-Saw Exercise - Descending>

Version 1: OH _____

etc.

LISTEN CAREFULLY. . .

Take time to listen to the examples of both exercises carefully before you try to sing them. They'll be much easier to perform if you have the pattern held clearly in your mind while you're singing.

Don't be surprised if your voice wants to wander all over the place in the beginning. This is quite natural. As you practice the see-saw exercises accurately, you'll gain control of your intensity of breath support, so that regardless of the pitches involved, your volume and quality will remain consistent.

CHAPTER 25

BREATHING FOR PHRASING

"The human voice remains the most moving, the most plastic, the most beautiful instrument that exists. Only the modern world seems to have forgotten that it is an instrument and that the singer, to achieve perfection, must fashion his or her instrument before attempting to play on it. This the average singer, even the average good singer, notoriously fails to do."

Francis Toye

KEEP AN EAR ON WHERE YOU'RE GOING

No discussion of phrasing is complete without talking about breathing. Breathing allows you to replenish the energy that gets you from Point A to Point B in a song. That's why singers must be acutely aware of how and when they're breathing. The "how" factor of breathing has been discussed in detail in the first section of this book and in Appendix #1. If you have any questions about the "how" of breathing, please re-read this material before going further.

To enter the realm of professional singing, it's as important to know *when* to breathe as *how* to breathe.

Here's a good exercise for practicing when to breathe. Take a song that you know fairly well and create a "road map" which indicates where to breathe in order to create the most pleasing phrasing. If you don't clearly map out where you need to breathe, the placement of your breathing can be haphazard. This results in the loss of phrasing consistency. When not breathing at regular intervals, singers often trap themselves into phrasings that are too long or create run-on sentences because they can't find a suitable place to breathe.

For example, if you're singing a rhythm and blues song and want to embellish it with the runs so often associated with this style, you *must* know when to take your breaths. If you don't, you may run out of breath before you get to the **riff** (another term for a group of notes added to the main melody to add interest and emotional punch to the tune). Even worse, you may run out of breath right in the middle of the run. As most singers can attest firsthand, this makes for a very anti-climactic moment in the song.

BREATHING WITH PUNCTUATION

To create your breathing "road map," first look at the sheet music of the song you want to sing. Punctuation marks (the marks found throughout all types of written material that indicate how words ought to be interpreted), will help you find sensible breathing points. Usually, a comma, period, or other punctuation mark will tell you where to pause and take a breath. If periods and commas are too numerous, you'll have to be selective so as not to break the music up too much.

Try not to breathe in the midst of a word, or in the middle of a complete thought when possible. The music will also give clues as to where to breathe. Sometimes, you'll have to negotiate between the lyrics and the music to find a breathing point that doesn't disturb either the flow of the music or the meaning of the lyrics.

Once you've identified where you want to take your breaths, mark them on the sheet music. This will guide your breathing, helping you to avoid careless breaths. Always use pencil when marking your sheet music, since breathing spots will change as your breath control and interpretive skills improve.

Following is "From a Distance" by Julie Gold, with the spots for breathing sensibly marked (each breathing point is marked with a check).

<Musical Example #11>

FROM A DISTANCE

Lyrics and Music by
JULIE GOLD

From a Distance - 4 - 1

From a Distance - 4 - 2

From a Distance - 4 - 3

Verse 2:
From a distance, we all have enough,
And no one is in need.
There are no guns, no bombs, no diseases,
No hungry mouths to feed.
From a distance, we are instruments
Marching in a common band;
Playing songs of hope, playing songs of peace,
They're the songs of every man.
(To Bridge:)

Verse 3:
From a distance, you look like my friend
Even though we are at war.
From a distance I just cannot comprehend
What all this fighting is for.
From a distance there is harmony
And it echos through the land.
It's the hope of hopes, it's the love of loves.
It's the heart of every man.

From a Distance - 4 - 4
5802FSMX

BASIC RULES FOR BREATHING

Use your own judgment in matters of breathing and where possible, use the following six guidelines to discover sensible breathing practices that can be studied using specific parts of the same song:

1) **Look Ahead** - Breathe in preparation for the entire sentence (or phrase) you're about to sing, not just the next note.

<Musical Example #12>

FROM A DISTANCE

Lyrics and Music by
JULIE GOLD

MUSICAL EXAMPLE #12 continued

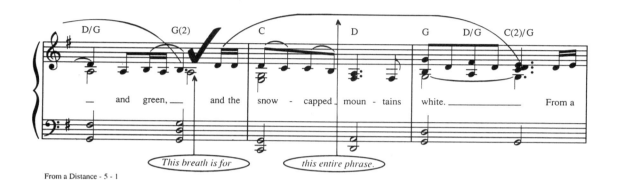

From a Distance - 5 - 1

2)   **End Phrases With A Bit Of Insurance** - You should never end a phrase completely out of air. A good exercise to add to your practice routine is to make it a habit to be able to sing any extended or difficult phrase twice on a breath, so that when you're performing, singing the same phrase once will be a breeze.

3)   **Don't Stop The Momentum** - Be sure not to slow down when you breathe. In tight spots, where there doesn't seem to be a place for even a quick sip, it's alright to borrow time from the last note of the phrase preceding the point where you need to breathe. Breaths should *never* delay the initiation of the upcoming phrase. These quick breaths are known as **catch** breaths. Be sure to keep them low and at belt level.

<Musical Example #13>

(The way you begin a phrase will determine how the entire phrase is sung - if you miss a breath at a critical moment, an entire phrase will be weakened.)

From a Distance - 5 - 3

4) **Just After A Breath, Hold Back A Bit Of Air -** Air is a lot like money: it's tricky to get and too easy to spend.

5) **Keep The Volume Consistent Before And After The Phrase** - Think of a breath as a hole in the flow of the line you're singing. Matching the volume before and after the breath is a characteristic of accomplished singing.

<Musical Example #14>

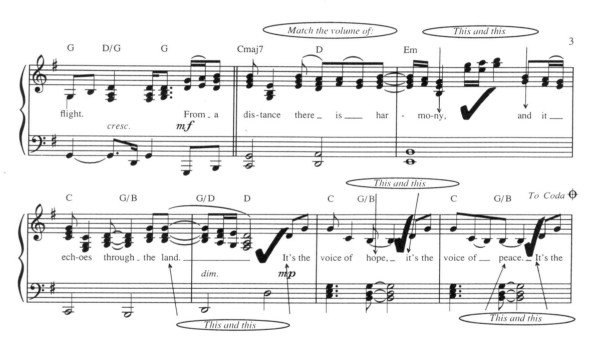

6) **Create Long Phrases Whenever Possible -** Longer phrases generally give a smoother, more connected sound to your singing. Breathe where it makes sense, according to the music and the lyrics. Use punctuation marks as a guide for your breathing points, but don't breathe at a punctuation mark unless you need to.

Musical Example #15 gives a version of "From A Distance" with a pattern of breathing that would result in short, choppy phrases. Compare this to the version in Musical Example #11 to see the difference. The phrasing of Example #11 would result in smooth, flowing lines and will definitely be a more "listenable" and professional rendition than that of Musical Example #15.

<Musical Example #15>

Incorrect breathing: Too many breaths

FROM A DISTANCE

Lyrics and Music by
JULIE GOLD

From a Distance - 4 - 1

From a Distance - 4 - 2

From a Distance - 4 - 3

5

Verse 2:
From a distance, we all have enough,
And no one is in need.
There are no guns, no bombs, no diseases,
No hungry mouths to feed.
From a distance, we are instruments
Marching in a common band;
Playing songs of hope, playing songs of peace,
They're the songs of every man.
(To Bridge:)

Verse 3:
From a distance, you look like my friend
Even though we are at war.
From a distance I just cannot comprehend
What all this fighting is for.
From a distance there is harmony
And it echos through the land.
It's the hope of hopes, it's the love of loves.
It's the heart of every man.

From a Distance - 4 - 4

CHAPTER 26

CONSONANTS

"The procedure for obtaining good diction can be easily stated: produce a pure vowel without distortion or "chewing," attach the proper consonants quickly and clearly, and move instantly into the next pure vowel sound."

William Rice
Basic Principles of Singing, 1961

CREATING A SEAMLESS LINE

Great singers move with tremendous agility from word to word, from vowel to vowel, *through* consonants. By definition, a consonant is "a sound produced by complete or partial blockage of the breath stream." A truly great singer will gently tap consonants into words with the touch of a feather.

But consonants are often the downfall of many would-be professional singers. Without proper training, phrasing may bump along due to the interference of bulky consonants.

THE PHYSICAL ELEMENT OF PHRASING

It's interesting to look at the similarity between a singer and a ventriloquist. The ventriloquist makes unbelievable sounds through exertion of the tongue, teeth and the roof of the mouth, while keeping the outer part of the mouth still. Singers are like ventriloquists in reverse, opening their mouths as much as possible, while the lips, tongue, and jaw move very little.

Both singer and ventriloquist are using parts of the mouth, called the **articulators,** but they're using them in different ways. If you want to create beautiful, flowing lines, unhindered by oversized consonants, you must keep the pathway of airflow clear whenever possible. This is accomplished by learning how to control the articulators.

The articulators include the roof of the mouth, the tongue, the upper and lower teeth and the lips (see Illustration #26.1).

ILLUSTRATION #26.1 - The Articulators

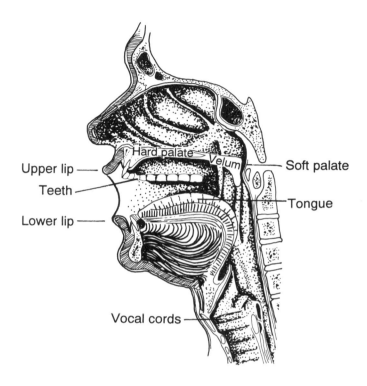

These parts of the mouth are used to shape consonants and vowels into words. The way you use the articulators will, to a large degree, determine the quality of your phrasing. For a more detailed explanation of the articulators, refer to Appendix 4.

If you've developed bad habits, such as allowing tension to dominate the mouth/jaw area or if you sing with exaggerated pronunciation, your consonants are most likely taking over your singing, with awkward phrasing as the result.

PASSION, YES; OVERDOING IT, NO!

Sometimes, singers with the most passion for their art are the ones who find the element of phrasing the most difficult. Why? Because they try *too hard.* Great singing sounds easy, and that's because professionals spend hours and hours working on the secrets of singing that lead to success.

But practice should not be confused with overdoing it. Although quality practice time requires a certain heat or intensity, forcing the cords into compliance will never accomplish anything. In your practice sessions, you should always be relaxed and comfortable. Then you can begin to mold tone into your "ideal" voice, as effort is reasonably applied.

Often what happens when singers are overly concerned about "succeeding" in singing is that over-pronunciation dominates their speech patterns. They literally try so hard to sing well that words are blown out of proportion.

As the consonants become larger and larger, vowels decrease in size until the articulators lock up. Don't confuse simple over-pronunciation with performing with true conviction and meaning.

OBSTACLES TO EASY SINGING

The vocal cords lie between the articulators and the breath support system. If you haven't developed strong breath control, the support muscles will blast air up from below, through the instrument. This is especially true when you're putting pressure on yourself to "succeed."

Combine this with articulators that are tense and locked up (due to oversized consonants), and you've got a major obstacle to easy singing. When too much air is being used and it can't move freely through the system and out through the mouth and nose, singing becomes nearly impossible.

Tension and overbearing, clumsy consonants cause serious problems in singers unaware of their impact on phrasing. If you remember the anatomy of the vocal cords (see Appendix 2), you know that the vocal cords' normal job is to resist the passage of air. When you're tense and/or over-enunciating, airflow is stopped by a constricted pathway and constricted articulators, trapping tone between the pressure from below and the overworked, tense mouth parts.

PUTTING YOUR CONSONANTS TO THE TEST

How do you know if you've overemphasized a consonant? Your tone provides the key. If you consistently produce rich, free-flowing tones on *vowels* in exercises such as those given in these pages, but suddenly experience thin tones, buzzing, unwanted raspiness, or vocal fatigue when singing songs, *consonants* most likely are the culprits.

The following Consonant Troubleshooting Guide lists the remedies for common problems that singers encounter with consonants.

FLAWS IN THESE SOUNDS	...HAPPEN WHEN...	HERE'S HOW TO FIX IT...
N, T, D, L	You press the tip of your tongue too hard against the roof of your mouth, behind the upper teeth.	Press your tongue against the roof of your mouth (*velum*) as if the velum was searingly hot. Pretend that if your tongue touched it for more than a brief instant, it would be burned.

CONSONANT TROUBLESHOOTING GUIDE

FLAWS IN THESE SOUNDS	...HAPPEN WHEN ...	HERE'S HOW TO FIX IT ...
M, P, B	You compress your lips too much. This causes air pressure to back up behind the lips until the lower support system has to blast them open, causing your throat and the tone to tighten.	Lightly compress the lips, then quickly release them to get open again to free the nearby vowels. If you hear a popping sound in the speakers when singing P or B into a microphone, you're pressing too hard. Decrease lip pressure until the popping sound disappears.
Q, K, C, NG, X, G (Hard G as in get)	You press the back of your tongue against the soft palate too firmly for too long. This inhibits airflow and creates extra pressure, which constricts the throat.	Think of these consonants as being lifted up and further forward in the mouth, on the front and downward slope of the pathway. Emphasize the vowel before and after the consonant to shorten the time it takes to sing these sounds.

CONSONANT TROUBLESHOOTING GUIDE		
FLAWS IN THESE SOUNDS	**...HAPPEN WHEN...**	**HERE'S HOW TO FIX IT...**
Y	You press your tongue too firmly against the soft palate. Tongue is tense.	Use relaxation exercises to loosen the tongue. Allow for only a small "Y."
J, G (soft G as in "George")	Your tongue squeezes up on the roof of the mouth too long or too hard.	Release any pressure in the tongue or lips. Make the sounds faster, smaller, lighter, and crisper. Use the tip of the tongue and front of the mouth only for the production of J and G. Don't get burned! (see N, T, D, L).
R	Don't hold your molars too close together when singing. This creates a compressed space in the back of your mouth and restricts the flow of tone.	Find a yawned "R" jaw position. Don't linger on the R: get off of it and move on to the next vowel. Pull your back molars apart as much as possible to create more space and unlock the R.

VOWELS VS. CONSONANTS?

Up to this point in the discussion of phrasing, consonants seem to be the bad guys. Vowels open the throat (the aim of all singers) and consonants constrict or close it altogether. But it's important to understand that vowels and consonants are not adversaries; you need both to create speech and song. The objective, therefore, is to learn how to apply the proper proportion of each.

One way to get the feeling of the correct proportion between vowels and consonants is to think of the vowels as the boxcars of a train. The boxcars (vowels) are linked together by connectors. These connectors are like consonants - they should be *very small* in relation to the size of the vowels (see Illustration #26.2).

ILLUSTRATION #26.2 -
Boxcars (Vowels) and Connectors (Consonants)

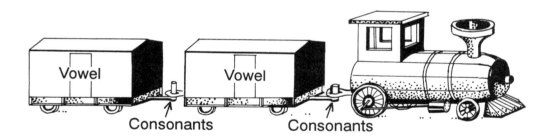

Often inexperienced singers *stress* consonants. They sing as if the train were made up of small boxcars and huge connectors. The result is the same as if you were riding on a train with squared off wheels - it's a rough, bumpy ride.

HOW CONSONANTS ASSIST FINDING FOCUS

The relationship between small consonants and big vowels can be very helpful in forming words correctly in the mouth for singing. When consonants are sung lightly, crisply, and on the tip of the tongue, near the teeth, this gives them a very frontalized or "forward in the mouth" feel. Vowels, on the other hand, fill the resonant spaces from the bottom of the throat, throughout the mouth, and up and out to the cheekbones.

When some consonants are correctly formed in this manner, their position is nearly the same as that of focus. A small, well-focused N, T, D, L, or S can be used as a guide for focus. While the body of vowels is anchored in the mouth, the head of each vowel is focused directly on the back of the top teeth, exactly where the mouth parts delicately gather to make the helpful consonants listed above.

LESS CONSONANT + MORE VOWEL = SMOOTH PHRASING

As in all artistic situations, there's a natural balance: when you take emphasis away from consonants, you have to put something back. In this case, put back greater reliance on vowels. Generally, a little more vowel and a little less consonant turns choppy singing into "singerly" lines of tone.

As you take emphasis off the consonant, you'll need to add strength via the support muscles to the vowels before and after the consonant. If you don't, the line of vowels itself will tend to sound weak.

Balancing vowels and consonants is always combined with keeping the pathway open and maintaining good, solid basic singing habits. One learns to blow air through the vowels and gently allow the consonants their place, without disturbing the line.

The more consonants that lurk in a word or phrase, the trickier your task becomes. The Singing on Vowels Only exercise of Chapter 23 will help you to overcome these challenges and, if practiced consistently, will lead to a new level of ease in singing.

FINAL CONSONANTS

When consonants occur as the last sound in a word, they can cause a closing off of the previous vowel. The most common of these "anticipated" sounds are R, N, and M. It's not unusual to hear a singer holding a note on one of these sounds. For instance, instead of sustaining the second syllable of the word heaven on the UH vowel sound (i.e., hea-vUHHHHHHHHH-n), it can be incorrectly sustained as hea-vUH-nnnnnnnnn! The word heart is often held as hearrrrrrrt rather than hAHHHHHHHHHrt.

Here are some other examples:

	Poorly Sung	**Correctly Sung**
heart	hearrrrrrt	h(AH)hhhhhhhhrt
heaven	heavennnnnn	h(EH)hhhhhhhven
flame	flammmmmmm	fl(EH)hhhhhheem
eyes	eyezzzzzzzzzz	(AH)hhhhhhhheez
times	Timmmmmmmz	t(AH)hhhhhheemz

Now take any exercise you've worked on up to this point and insert some of the consonants from the Consonant Troubleshooting Guide before each note.

VOICED AND UNVOICED CONSONANTS

As with vowels, there's more to consonants than meets the eye. Some consonants are **voiced** - these consonants have a slight "buzz" or "hum" when spoken or sung. B, G, L, and V are examples of voiced consonants. There are also **voiceless** or **unvoiced** consonants. On sounds such as F, T, H, K, P, and S, there's no hummed sound or vibration produced with the consonant. To really hear the difference between the two types of consonants, plug one or both ears (as you did in the Focus Chapter) and produce a voiced consonant followed by an unvoiced consonants. There's an unmistakable difference between the two.

Voiced consonants, because they contain a vibration of the cord, actually *assist* in maintaining the through-line of a phrase. If the ideal is a line of vowels with no breaks at all, the next best thing is to have a line of vowels broken up by voiced consonants, since the vibration, though it will vary within the line, will be sustained even in these consonants.

The risk with unvoiced consonants is that by their very nature, they stop or cause a break in the line of tone. When the vibration is cut off, breath, focus and line are often lost, causing a breakdown of the phrase. As a result, breath control suffers and too much air comes into play and tone will crack or sound strident.

For example, if you sing "These are the Best of Times . .," it's the vowel after the T that's at risk. If that "T" happens to come in the middle of a line of words, *the whole passage, until you take your next breath, may suffer.* Unvoiced consonants are worthy of special attention when they occur in the middle of phrases sung in the upper range. A strong sense of breath control automatically cuts down consonants to the proper size. Good singing habits balance consonants and vowels automatically.

ACCENTUATE THE POSITIVE

The best way to sing the unvoiced consonants is to make them as small as possible, getting to the following vowel as rapidly as you can. It's really a matter, as always, of emphasizing the vowels and de-emphasizing the consonants. The unvoiced consonants (which are basically all air and no vibration) deserve your closest scrutiny.

There's another useful way to handle the unvoiced troublemakers. That's through the use of **consonant modifications**. Here's how it works. Basically, it's a matter of adjusting unvoiced consonants towards their voiced cousins. If you sing a word in the *upper voice* and it contains a T, as in "best of times," sing the T's as if they were D's. D is the voiced version of T, that is, the articulators work the same, but there's tone added: D buzzes in the throat, where T doesn't. Thus, "bes(d) of (d)imes" is easier to sing than "best of times" in the middle of a phrase in the upper voice.

This technique can only be used in the upper range (in the low to mid-range, the modification is too obvious); however, practicing these modifications will increase your awareness of consonants throughout your range.

There are many similar cases. For example, P does not buzz in the throat (it's an unvoiced consonant), *but B does.* So when you're singing in the upper extension, if you change the P's to B's, there's a much better chance of staying focused. Using the following Consonant Modification Charts as your guide, practice these consonant modifications in songs and exercises until they become second nature.

There are a few other sounds, such as H and W, that don't have any substitutes, so make them very small, very quick and get to the vowel as soon as possible. Consonant modifications should be made delicately. They should *never* be obvious. Examine the following Consonant Modification Charts closely to see how these sounds may be adjusted to insure they don't disrupt smooth singing lines.

CONSONANT MODIFICATIONS

Modify this unvoiced consonant. . .	. . .to this voiced consonant:
F	V
P	B
S	Z
T	D
C (cat)	G
Q (quiet)	G

MODIFICATIONS FOR COMPOUND CONSONANTS

Compound consonants containing two or three unvoiced consonants are common in lyrics. If these cases occur in the high voice, you can modify them all at once.

COMPOUND CONSONANT MODIFICATIONS

Modify these compound consonants	. . .to these compound consonants:
ST	ZD
STR	ZDR
SP	ZB

EXERCISE #32: ASCENDING ARPEGGIO FOR CONSONANT MODIFICATIONS

Now try these modifications out on the following exercise. Sing an arpeggio up to the octave note. On the first three notes of the arpeggio, use an unvoiced consonant. Then, on the fourth, or octave note, switch to a voiced consonant. This will prepare you to think of a consonant modification at a moment's notice. In musical notation, this exercise looks like this:

<Musical Example>

Version 1: TAH TAH TAH DAH

Be sure to listen to the musical example on the CD, so that you've got the idea clearly in mind.

The sample of lyrics below is taken from Dennis DeYoung's "The Best of Times," © 1981, Stygian Songs. The words of the chorus are:

**The Best of Times
Are when I'm alone with you
Some rain, some shine
We'll make this a world for two**

Sung with the consonant modifications for the words in the upper range, improve the flow of the lines by singing them as follows:

The (M)est of (D)imes
Are When I'm Alone With You
(Z)ome rain, (z)ome shine
We'll ma(g) thi(z) a world (v)or (d)wo

Use your sense of musicality to determine how much to modify the consonant. Obviously, if the words of the song become obscured, you're overdoing it or you're modifying consonants in the middle range where the changes are too obvious. In any case, practice the modifications until your phrasing is smooth and free-flowing (in a word, it should sound "easy" to your audience). Simply "thinking in" the modifications while singing the actual consonants provides the best way to insure that too much change is not affecting words

Here's the whole song with advice for breath marks, 1/2 H's, and vowel and consonant modifications notated.

<Musical Example #16: The Best of Times>

The Best Of Times - 6 - 1

No modification - not enough time. A note has to last at least one full beat in the music to be able to be modified.

The Best Of Times · 6 - 2

The Best Of Times · 6 · 3

The Best Of Times - 6 - 4

The Best Of Times - 6 - 5

The Best Of Times - 6 - 6

PART FIVE:

GENERAL REFERENCE

CHAPTER 27

VOICE TYPES

"... the greatest obstacle in the artistic development of an actor (or singer) is HASTE - the forcing of his immature powers..."

Constantin Stanislavski
from E. Herbert Caesari's
The Alchemy of Voice

THE FOUR BASIC VOICE TYPES

Voices, male and female, differ in range and quality. The range is not the only factor in determining the kind of voice; *timbre* (tone quality or color) is equally important.

Every singer should eventually know with certainty what type of voice he or she has. There are four basic voice types from highest to lowest: *soprano, mezzo-soprano (or alto), tenor, and bass*. The first two are female voices and the latter two are male.

These four voice types can be expanded to include five and sometimes six standard voice categories that are used by songwriters, stage directors, conductors and bands. They are: *soprano, mezzo-soprano, contralto, tenor, baritone, and bass.* Further subdivisions are also used when discussing the quality of voices sometimes found within each of the six major categories.

FEMALE VOICE CLASSIFICATIONS

Sopranos are named not only for their differing timbres, but also for the type of music which suits their range, voice quality, and technical ability.

The Soprano Voice

Singing in the highest range of all sopranos (and in the opera world, often without words) is the *coloratura soprano*. A *coloratura* is an embellishment of a melody, an ornament. A coloratura singer specializes in highly ornate arias and songs and uses a lighter sound than the dramatic or lyric soprano.

The coloratura was previously used mostly in the opera world. Things have changed, however, with the popularization of *scatting* and *melisma.* Scatting, used mostly in jazz music, is improvisation on one-syllable sounds, which have no meaning, that is, they're not full words. Melisma (ornamentation of an especially elaborate or emotional type) is practiced most often by gospel singers. These improvised runs have found their way into many styles of popular music. Contemporary vocal music, in general, has become more highly ornamented. In fact, it's not just high soprano voices anymore, but all voice types (male and female), that have taken to adding ornamental embellishments to songs. Often, these runs are borrowed from great instrumentalists, both past and present.

The most familiar of the soprano voices is the *lyric soprano.* The repertoire of a lyric soprano consists of compositions whose melodies are in the upper range, and often contain quite a few *runs*.

A soprano with a somewhat lower extension is the *mezzo-soprano.* The "mezzo-soprano" shares nearly the range and qualities of the lyric soprano while having extra power in the lower range. One of the most famous mezzo-soprano roles in opera is Carmen.

The *dramatic soprano* (in Italian, spinto), a deeper and more powerful voice, is sometimes less comfortable with ornate runs. This voice type gives the overall impression of an earthier tone than the fluid sounds of the lyric soprano, but also can span quite a range, using the extreme top and bottom of the voice.

The Contralto Voice

The lowest of the female voices, the *contralto,* can be called upon to sing in the *tessitura* (predominant range) below middle C. (The tessitura is the general "lie" of a vocal part, whether high or low in pitch.) The timbre of the contralto voice is usually darker and thicker than the other female voice types. There's no mistaking a true contralto (which is actually quite rare). This type of voice sounds rich, warm and attractive to the ear and resounds with a wonderful depth of tone.

MALE VOICE CLASSIFICATIONS

The Tenor Voice

The highest of the male voices is the ***tenor*** voice, which has two main textures: lyric and dramatic. A ***lyric tenor*** is most comfortable when singing long, melodious lines which don't require a consistently heavy tone quality. Many of the most famous popular bands and singers have been lyric tenors. Steve Perry, Freddie Mercury, Stevie Wonder, Paul McCartney and Sting fit into this type of voice classification.

The ***dramatic tenor*** has a similar range to the lyric tenor but can last much longer singing very loud with a heavy timbre or quality.

The Baritone Voice

One of the favorites among male voices is the ***baritone***. Like mezzo-sopranos, the range of a baritone lies between two of the other voices, bass and tenor. Though often more lyric in nature, baritones may be dramatic as well, with very powerful, booming low tones which share tenorial splendor on top and the basses' solemnity on the bottom.

The Bass Voice

Basses, of course, are the lowest of all the voice categories. Bass singers are very important to all harmony singing groups and have always held a special place in the hearts of music lovers everywhere.

WHAT'S YOUR VOICE TYPE?

For the purposes of this book, it's really not necessary to know your exact voice type; just practice with the accompanying CD that feels most comfortable to you; in fact, trying to classify your voice in the beginning can cause confusion. It takes an experienced ear to detect the subtle qualities that determine the classification of voices. While there are some voices that are easily classified, some require great care and judgment to determine their type.

Wait and See

It's important to let the voice unfold and reveal it's type over a period of time. Finding your true vocal classification is one of the major decisions you'll make (hopefully with the aid of an experienced voice specialist) in your study of singing.

But be cautious: correct vocal typing can't always be done at the first hearing of your instrumental characteristics. Sometimes, it takes time to correct improper singing habits and concepts before a true assessment can be made. It's a serious mistake to jump the gun and label your voice just for the sake of calling it something.

When a voice is wrongly classified, a great deal of time is lost. You end up struggling to sing material that's ill-suited for your voice. The result is usually the development of a technique and sound that's as confusing to an audience as it is to you.

Many students spend months (or years) trying to undo bad habits that were acquired because they tried to sing music that just wasn't compatible with their voice type.

THE VOICE KNOWS BEST

The best course of action is to leave the voice alone long enough to let the instrument tell you what it is. If you proceed with competent and consistent training, your vocal quality, range and location of the **passaggio** (the notes where upper middle tones join with those of the highest reaches of the voice), will allow for a proper vocal analysis.

Inevitably, there will be a few cases of legitimate re-classification. This may occur, for instance, as the voice matures with age, resulting in changes in vocal color and range. Sometimes poor training replaced by effective vocal training can be the basis of a reclassification. Historically, this has often happened where a baritone moves up to tenor territory or vice-versa.

But, for the most part, if you work patiently with a voice teacher, you'll be able to make a determination of lasting value. This important decision will help you choose a **repertoire** (songs maintained for auditions, performances and recording) that's appropriate to your voice, allowing for a safe and healthy study of singing. Illustration #27.1 shows the ranges of five of the most commonly referred to voice types as they relate to the piano keyboard.

ILLUSTRATION #27.1 - The Ranges of
Voice Types Described On A Keyboard

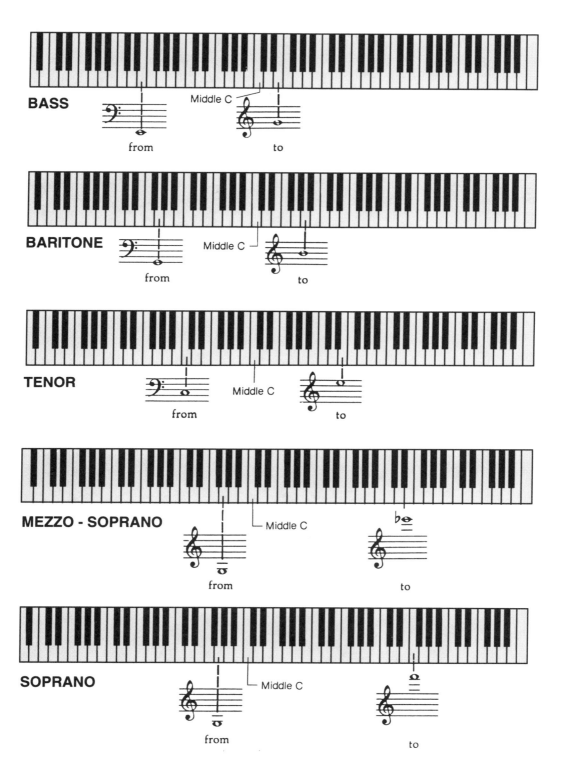

CHAPTER 28

POSTURE: AN ESSENTIAL FOR VOCAL FREEDOM

"Fate is being kind to me. Fate doesn't want me to be too famous too young."

Duke Ellington

GOOD POSTURE PAYS BIG DIVIDENDS

Posture plays an important role in all of the performing arts, but especially in singing, acting and dancing. *When singing, you can't breathe properly unless you have good posture.* It's that simple. You can practice the breathing exercises in this book or breath exercises from other sources until you're blue in the face, but you still won't acquire good breathing habits unless your posture is correct.

On top of the technical benefits of good posture, it also makes you look your best as you perform; it signals to your audience that you're confident and that you're not afraid to stand behind your performance and give it your all.

Some people come by good posture naturally. Most of us, however, need to pay attention to our habitual postures, and make adjustments, as necessary. Posture is especially important for singers who started as guitarists, bassists, drummers or pianists. Instrumentalists tend to use inadequate posture habits while practicing slumped over their instruments for hours on end.

Poor posture can lead to big singing problems. However, these problems often cease when you learn correct singing posture.

GOOD POSTURE ISN'T JUST "STANDING UP STRAIGHT"

When most people think about "good" posture, they think of "stomach in, chest out, shoulders back!" Their stance is very rigid and very tense. This kind of "military" posture will undermine your singing every bit as much as a slouched position.

So exactly what is the proper posture for singing? Here's a complete rundown, from head to toe.

PHOTO #28.1 - Correct and Incorrect Singing Postures (a) (b) (Standing)

a) Correct   b.) Incorrect

Feet

The feet form the **base** on which your whole instrument stands balanced (see Illustration #28.1). To establish a correct base:

✔ Stand with feet shoulder-width apart, one foot a little ahead of the other.

✔ Put the weight of your body somewhat forward on the balls of your feet (not back on the heels).

✔ Make sure the weight is evenly distributed.

With this stance, you'll feel firmly planted on the ground. These simple guidelines will help you avoid some of the most common mistakes: leaning forward on one foot, on the back of your heels, or swaying nervously while you sing. While these errors might seem harmless, they **telegraph** or signal to your audience that you're unsure of yourself.

Telegraphing is the tendency to lift up or tense an area just before you sing an upper note or difficult passage. Not only does it make singing more difficult, it exposes your weaknesses. It tells your audience that you're worried about an upcoming note, for instance.

ILLUSTRATION #28.1 - Proper Position of the Feet When Singing

Correct   Incorrect   Incorrect

Legs

There's just one thing to remember about the leg area, but it's very important: **don't lock your knees.** Keep the legs relaxed, and the knees very slightly bent.

Hips

Stand with your hips resting comfortably and evenly on your legs. Other characteristics of correct singing posture are:

✔ Your hips should face the audience, not jut out to one side.

✔ As with the knees, don't rigidly lock the pelvis into an unnatural position - don't tilt the pelvis up or backwards (unless you're working with a specialist to solve a specific problem).

✔ Don't position the hips too far forward over the toes, or too far back behind the heels.

Back and Spine

To achieve good posture in the back and spine, try this simple, effective technique used by Van Christy in his book <u>Foundations in Singing</u>.

1. Imagine an elastic band attached to your heels. Picture it running up through the legs, spine, and neck, and coming out through the top of your head (see Photo #28.2a).

2. Raise your arms straight up over your head, "grab" the elastic band, and give it an imaginary tug. This will pull your chest up into position, and the hips, torso, neck and head into alignment (see Photo #28.2b).

3. Now stretch your arms out, and let them drop *slowly* to your sides (see Photo #28.2c).

4. As your arms come down, your chest and shoulders will fall into a good natural position in relation to the back and spine (see Photo #28.2d).

PHOTO #28.2 (a) (b) (c) (d) - Elastic Band Exercise

a)   b)   c)   d)

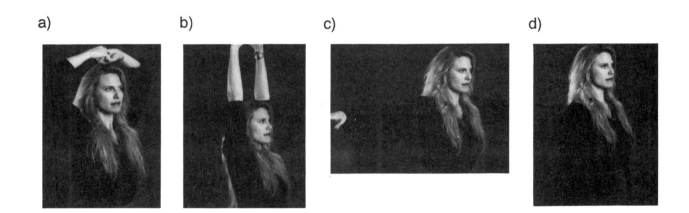

Chest

The experts are divided as to how the chest should be carried. Some vocal teachers say to raise it high. Others advocate lifting the ribs and holding them in this awkward position while singing.

If you combine the results of the previous exercise with the guidelines outlined in the "Breathing: Less Is More" and "Mastering Breathing" chapters, your chest will settle into a comfortable position automatically.

It's important to keep the weight of your chest off the lower breath support system. Just remember to:

✔ Keep your spine upright (using the elastic band exercise); and

✔ Keep your shoulders in position (see the next section to learn how).

Shoulders

There are two key words to remember for the shoulders: *level and relaxed.* The natural, relaxed position for the shoulders is downward and backward (see Illustration #28.2). If you feel tension in the shoulders, don't try to force them to relax. Just take a deep breath, and let them settle into a comfortable position. If you're still having problems relaxing your shoulders, try this:

✔ Raise both arms straight out in front, palms down.

✔ Now rotate them in a wide arching movement, up over the head, back behind, and then down to your sides.

✔ Shake your shoulder joints so they don't become too rigid. (As you shake, make sure the weight of your chest is comfortably up off your ribs and lower breath support muscles.)

Now check your shoulders. This movement should have put them into a good, solid singing position.

Never let your shoulders lift up when you inhale. This creates tension in the upper torso which interferes with good breathing.

ILLUSTRATION #28.2 - Position of Chest and Shoulder

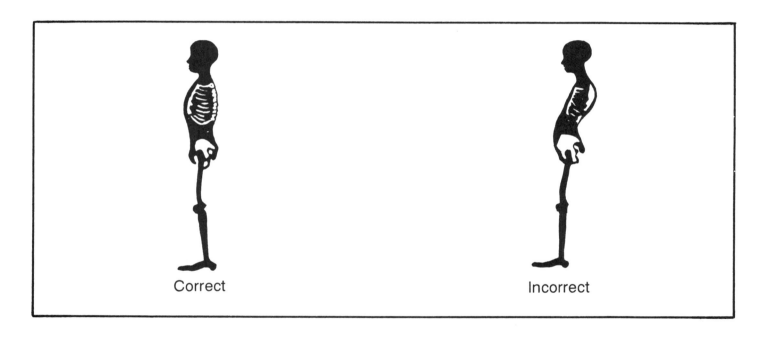

Correct   Incorrect

Neck and Head

The neck is one of the biggest problem areas for singers (both beginners and professionals).

Because of many misconceptions about singing, inexperienced singers tend to sing *into or from* the throat, rather than simply allowing tone to pass *through* the throat. The resulting tension and constricted pathway become a major obstacle to good singing.

What can you do to keep tension out of the neck area? One of the major keys to a relaxed neck is to keep your jaw line level (parallel to the ground - see Illustration #28.3). Sometimes singers jut out the chin, especially during emotional passages. This also creates tension in the neck area, and detracts from your performance.

ILLUSTRATION #28.3 - Jaw Positions

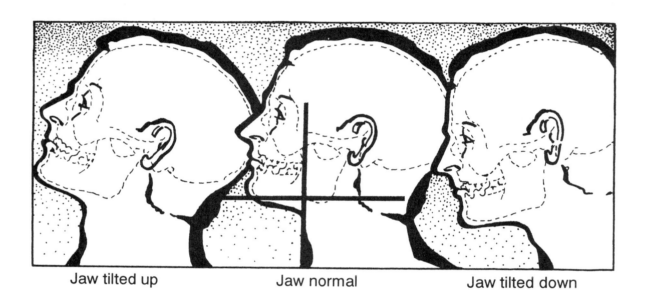

Jaw tilted up   Jaw normal   Jaw tilted down

By keeping your Point of View (P.O.V.) down, you'll most likely influence your head to stay properly aligned. With the head tilted too far up, the singer can seem aloof or haughty to the audience. Turned down, the vocalist is often perceived as being somewhat embarrassed.

Keep in mind that the gesture or body language of your head counts. So try to sing with the head in a neutral position, neither too far up nor too far down. This also alleviates the added tension on the voice box, which can result in a "pinched," cut-off tone (see Photos #28.3 a, b, c).

PHOTOS# 28.3: (a) (b) (c) Positions of the Head

a)

b)

c)

Too High

Correct

Too Low

Arms and Hands

Singers often make overly dramatic use of their hands. In the extreme, this can make an otherwise competent performance look ridiculous. In general, singers use their hands too much and raise them too high. They don't realize how this upstages or steals interest away from their singing.

In general, allow your arms and hands to hang comfortably at your sides. When you do move your hands, keep the movement mostly low around belt level, until you reach the climax of the song. Then, and only then, should you feel free to use more dramatic and higher gestures.

BE SPONTANEOUS

When performing, avoid pre-planning or "choreographing" your hand movements. This is easy to do when you've developed a solid vocal technique, which enables you to put aside technical worries and deal with songs on an emotional level. Your hands will automatically follow the feelings you express in your singing. More importantly, they'll convey the emotion as a natural extension of your performing style.

Spontaneous gestures make for an honest and unique performance. It's far better to express yourself in that way than insert pre-programmed gestures into your act. The great dancer, Margot Fonteyn, stated it best "Great artists are people who find the way to be themselves in their art. Any sort of . . .[false appearance] . . . induces mediocrity in art and life alike."

SOME RULES FOR SINGING WHEN SITTING

Needless to say, poor sitting posture is as undesirable as poor standing posture (see Photo #28.4 a & b) When sitting, observe the same guidelines as for standing, with the following modifications:

✔ Find the front edge of the chair and use that as the base of your support structure (your support structure now being the bottom of your pelvis, rather than your feet).

✔ Maintain a straight spine, with your body tilted slightly forward and away from the chair. Don't get *too* comfortable with the position of your spine (but don't make yourself too rigid, either). Don't bow your spine in the opposite direction in an effort to sit up straight.

✔ Keep your feet planted flat on the ground. Don't lean on the upper part of the chair or wrap your arms around it.

✔ Don't slip back, allowing your bottom to fill the entire area of the chair. If you do, you're sure to slouch, and cause your spine to bow in an outward semi-circle. This limits the movement of your diaphragm and ribs while you breathe.

PHOTO #28.4 (a) (b) - Sitting Posture

a) Correct   b) Incorrect

CHAPTER 29

PRACTICE GUIDE

"It is simplicity that emerges with all its charm, as the final seal upon art. Whoever hopes to attain this quickly will never achieve it, one cannot begin at the end. One must have studied, even immensely, to reach this goal, and it is not easy...."

Chopin

A CHECKLIST FOR SERIOUS STUDENTS OF SINGING

Here's a list of guidelines that will help you organize your practice time effectively. If you can't practice long on any given day, do breath work (the Controlled Release exercise and Messa di Voce) *instead* of singing exercises or songs. It's always better to have a good, strong breathing session than to sing frantically for twenty minutes.

Warm Up Before You Practice

A little light, outdoor exercise before starting vocal practice is always beneficial. Sit-ups and leg lifts are also ideal exercises for this purpose (see Illustration #29.1). Not only do they warm you up, but they strengthen the muscles of the lower breath support system as well.

Try to do 20 or 30 repetitions each of both sit-ups and leg lifts to wake up your lower breathing muscles; then do 25 to 100 jumping jacks to bring the full body up to speed.

ILLUSTRATION #29.1 - Sit-ups and Leg Lifts

Sit-ups

Leg lifts

One last word of caution: whatever exercise you choose, go easy; don't fatigue yourself. Gently work your body up to the physical state of exhilaration. *Then you're truly ready to practice, mentally and physically.*

Relaxation Is Essential

If you've been talking throughout the day or have been preoccupied with matters other than singing, spend ten or fifteen minutes "focusing" before beginning serious practicing. The voice tends to fall down out of focus and can be worn to a frazzle when speech patterns are far below the mask, and unsupported.

If your workday has fatigued you or you feel worn out mentally, allow yourself to lie still on a couch until you feel rested, mind *and* body. Singing when you're tired is a losing battle and usually just leads to a frustrating practice session. After relaxing, re-energize your body and mind with some light physical exercises.

The body should be trained to react quickly to the warming up procedure. A quick check on posture, some deep breathing and a few of your favorite relaxation techniques ought to get you on your way. Don't become discouraged if the first five minutes of practice doesn't sound great. The first five or ten minutes of work should be free of evaluation or critical analysis. The voice will respond quicker if you allow it to warm up under non-critical circumstances.

If frustration overcomes patience, stop singing for awhile and come back to it after a walk, shower, or other diversion. Don't press your endurance or your patience past the breaking point. But watch out here! Sometimes the breakthrough you're seeking lies just beyond the point where most people would give up. Difficult exercises should be left for last, when the voice feels up for them.

Practicing In The Car

Here's a word to those of you whose normal practice routine consists mainly of getting in your car, switching on the radio, tape or CD and singing along with your favorite artists. **Be careful!**

Most of the time when you're driving, you're tense, not warmed up and straining to sing over traffic and engine noise. This is by no means a good singing environment. Inevitably, you're going to be unprepared for "high" notes and other challenges that occur in the music you're singing along with. If it's the only place available to you for practice, use it. When better practice situations are available, use them instead. The car can work, but use common sense.

PHOTO #29.1 - Performance Shot

THE FOLLOWING TEN-STEP POWER VOCAL WORK-OUT IS A COLLECTION OF PROVEN STEPS THAT WILL HELP YOU OPTIMIZE YOUR REHEARSAL TIME. SINGING TO THE BEST OF YOUR ABILITY EACH TIME YOU WORK IS AN IMPORTANT HABIT TO CULTIVATE. DON'T EVER "KIND OF" SING.

RELAX! RELAX! AND THEN RELAX AGAIN. FOLLOW THE ROUTINES AS DESCRIBED IN THE RELAXATION EXERCISES OR MAKE UP YOUR OWN.

TEN-STEP
POWER VOCAL WORK-OUT

Getting Ready to Sing

1. Be sure you're physically awake and alert. Do some light calisthenics, take a walk, or whatever activity wakes up your muscles and gives you a general feeling of well-being.

   ❏ Establish good posture (see chapter on Posture).

   ❏ Be sure your neck, shoulders, jaw and tongue are relaxed. Use the relaxation exercises in Part One to be sure.

2. Repeat the Controlled Release and Pressure Release breath exercises until the breath muscles feel warmed up and flexible.

Warming Up the Instrument

3. Hum (with open throat).

4. Practice Vocal Exercises 1 - 6.

5. Sing through the first endurance group, striving for:

❏ Even vowels
❏ Focused and anchored tone
❏ Pathway (the beginning of that yawn sensation!)
❏ Smooth initiation
❏ Pure vowels
❏ Correct tongue position and P.O.V.
❏ Sensation of elevation - "smiling" tones

Inviting in the Upper Range

6. Sing through the second endurance group, striving for those qualities described in #5:

❏ Also try out crisp, quick, voiced and unvoiced consonants. Try to move air through the instrument using the lower breath support muscles, with as little interference from the non-vowel sounds as possible.

❏ Use a mirror to be sure there's no tension gathering in the face, neck, jaw or shoulders.

❏ Listen to yourself breathe. Are your breaths quiet? Can you sense each top note moving through the tall back end of the reversed megaphone and out through the small hole-in-the-wall at the front end?

❏ Does the megaphone's angle stay steadily down in front as you ascend by scale or leap through the upper range? Are you using your diaphragm to *prevent* too much air from hitting the cords?

7. Use your discretion to add or delete exercises as necessary to accommodate the amount of time you have to practice. It's not necessary to do each exercise or all repetitions each time you practice. If your time is limited, make up a routine out of the exercises collected in this book that suits your schedule.

8. Messa di Voce

9. Select from Exercises 13 - 15, 21 - 23, 29 - 32, depending on what techniques you wish to emphasize at this particular practice session.

10. Endurance Group Three

PHOTO #29.2 - Student Practicing With Mirror

LONG TERM PRACTICING SUGGESTIONS

If you're not in the mood to sing, do something else (take a walk, shower, or read an inspiring book) that makes you want to sing. A professional is not someone who is always in the mood to sing, but rather someone who has learned how to consistently create conditions in his or her life that makes quality singing possible.

Create a lifestyle for yourself that promotes the desire to sing each day. Though challenging for some vocalists at first, this is a sensible long-term project.

Eventually, you'll notice how much easier it is to sing when you feel happy and cheerful than when you're angry, unhappy, bored or lazy. The voice is very difficult to move up and out through the pathway when you're out-of-sorts with the world. When practice or performance time is near, begin by humming lightly with a feeling of the beginning of a yawn in the throat. This is a good starting point for tone before actually singing exercises or songs.

The feel of the "hum" should be at the anchor points around the nose and mouth, with sympathetic resonance deep in the throat and chest. Early in the day, move the sense of vocal placement to the mouth, where brilliance can be combined with the natural depth daybreak brings to most singers' tone.

CHAPTER 30

VOICE MAINTENANCE

"Singing is 95% brains, 95% talent, 95% perseverance and 95% guts!"

Jerome Hines

MAINTAINING VOCAL HEALTH

The various parts of the voice make up one of the most delicate mechanisms of the human body. Given that reliability as a vocal professional will be valued as much as talent, be aware there is a relationship between good health, sensible vocal maintenance and consistent performance quality.

Proper diet, exercise, and rest are essential for the overall well-being of the instrument. Going overboard or neglecting any one of these areas *now and then* never stopped anyone from becoming a professional. Chronic abuse or disregard, on the other hand, can and has stopped or shortened the careers of many would-be singers.

USE COMMON SENSE TO CARE FOR YOUR VOICE

Good health requires sensible living habits. Combined with a powerful technique, like the one outlined in these pages, a singer is much less likely to succumb to the ailments and vocal problems experienced by a vocalist who relies on luck and vocal myths.

For the singer, more than anything else, it's important to live as normal a life as possible, always taking into consideration that you take your instrument with you wherever you go. Don't worry needlessly, but do be aware of the general requirements of vocal health.

The following is a description of some of the most common problems singers face in maintaining good vocal health. The subjects listed are by no means exhaustive, but should serve to generally inform the student and professional alike regarding effective vocal health maintenance.

PHOTO #30.1 - Performance Shot

COLDS AND LARYNGITIS

The most familiar curse to singers is the "cold" that somehow they're always either "just getting" or "just getting over." The best preventative medicine for the common cold is to maintain overall superior health habits.

The body's first line of defense - the immune system - is greatly affected by your general lifestyle and mental outlook. Tension and depression break down the system, so you should do whatever it takes to maintain a positive outlook and minimize stress.

Is It Harmful To Sing When You Have A Cold?

It's okay to sing with a cold, as long as it's not a severe cold (i.e., it hasn't progressed to the point where the cords are involved). If your singing habits are correct, you may experience some discomfort, but you won't injure your voice.

If you have a slight head cold, and you have to sing, work hard for the feel of the voice being "elevated" out of the throat via the inner smile, or the concept of 90%/10%, as described in Chapter 4, Elevating the Voice. These techniques can be extremely helpful when you need to sing with a slight cold.

It's a completely different matter, however, if the cold is in the throat and is exhibiting characteristics associated with **laryngitis** (where the vocal cords are swollen and inflamed). Laryngitis is an infection of the vocal cords and is a serious malady. In this case, singing, as well as speech, will be difficult and you may jeopardize the heart of the instrument, the vocal cords, if you use the voice under these conditions. When you have laryngitis, the only remedy is rest from singing and speaking for as long as it takes for the ailment to subside. Check with your doctor to see if any prescription medication would be appropriate for your condition.

When your speaking voice returns, you can begin to build up, little by little (over several days to several weeks) to your normal practice or performance schedule.

SMOKING INJURES THE VOICE

Smoking, whether it be tobacco or any other substance, should be absolutely avoided! In addition, avoid inhaling secondhand smoke in nightclubs, restaurants, your workplace or at home. Of course, there are situations where you won't have control over the environment. However, whenever possible, it's to your advantage to do whatever it takes to avoid inhaling cigarette smoke and other irritants to the vocal apparatus.

Any form of recreational drug use should also be *strictly avoided*. Though often romanticized by movies, magazines, and advertising, the truth is that *any* type of smoking, or other drug usage, is simply out of the question. It's going to harm your instrument and self-confidence as well as your body, in general. It's just too much to risk.

Smoking dries the membranes of the throat and irritates the entire vocal mechanism. The continued influence of heat, nicotine, ash, formaldehyde, acetylene (a chemical used in welding!), acetone (more commonly known as nail polish remover) and other harmful chemicals can affect the cords until your tone becomes irreparably husky and rough.

The bottom line is, if you smoke, you're endangering your entire career. Smoking can cause *irreparable* damage to the membranes of the throat, nasal passages and vocal cords. If you've never had a strong enough reason to quit smoking, this is it. Smoking will prohibit you from ever knowing just how great your talent really is.

PHOTO #30.2 - Performance Shot

WHAT ABOUT ALCOHOL?

Singers often drink a glass of wine or a beer before or during a performance to "loosen up." Since relaxation is a critical aspect of good singing, it seems to follow that if you have just a drink or two before performing, you'll sing better. However, while you may *feel* less tense after a drink, your muscular (and mental) coordination, as well as your capacity to evaluate your performance, are somewhat reduced.

On the physical level, alcohol dilates the capillaries in the vocal cords, and can cause an excessive production of mucus, which is irritating to say the least. Often, singers complain of a dry throat after a "warm-up" drink. The best advice as far as combining drinking and singing goes is: *don't do it*, especially just before or during a performance.

Singers are naturally sensitive and excitable people. Alcohol *undermines* their sense of well-being, as opposed to creating an exaggerated sense of competence and confidence. If you're really serious about singing, there's simply no place for anything more than occasional, well-timed, sensible consumption of alcoholic beverages.

Don't Smoking and Drinking
Give Your Voice A Good Rock 'N' Roll Sound?

A popular myth among rock singers is that smoking and drinking help to achieve a rough, husky quality, often seen as desirable for rock 'n' roll. However, the risks far outweigh the gains. Interestingly enough, some singers seem to have a lasting and naturally gritty quality, almost an in-born capacity to achieve a husky tone, with or without smoking and drinking. But, if this isn't the case with you, and your voice takes a beating whenever you use the "gritty" sound, don't push yourself over the edge of vocal common sense.

Most singers who use alcohol and/or smoking to instill some character into their voice simply end up with no voice at all. Building a solid technique and working on the emotional aspects of songs, as well as gaining more experience onstage and in the studio will work much more effectively to achieve the same results. The only difference is that the latter method won't cause permanent voice damage, loss of high notes, or calloused cords (which, by the way, can require surgery).

ALLERGIES AND THROAT IRRITATIONS

Many singers habitually clear their throats. In some cases, this can be attributed to habit. In others, it's related to allergies. Often, singers who suffer from mild to severe allergy attacks don't even know the problem exists and that it's highly treatable. Allergies can affect the tissues of the throat, nose, and ears, including the most disturbing sensation of having mucus drainage, onto the vocal cords.

In cases where allergies are mild enough to be only a temporary and sporadic disturbance, a solid technique will often offset the minor irritation caused by this condition. However, if you have serious, pervasive allergic reactions frequently, you'll require treatment by a throat specialist. If you need to clear your throat often, over an extended period of time, you're risking your vocal health.

In any case, singers need to learn to clear their throats delicately, using the diaphragm rather than harshly scraping the cords together. Coughing should also be controlled and as gentle as possible. A hacking cough should be taken seriously. Use common sense and over-the-counter remedies (sparingly), when necessary, to calm the cough reflex, and to avoid battering the vocal mechanism. If the cough persists, see a throat specialist.

PHOTO #30.3 - Performance Shot

EXERCISE HELPS YOUR SINGING TREMENDOUSLY

Exercise and sports are a great asset to maintaining high health standards and low tension levels for the singer. Aerobic exercises, calisthenics and stress reduction methods such as yoga or T'ai Chi, are especially suitable for overall mind and body fitness.

As with everything else, exercise should be done in moderation. Never exercise to exhaustion - that just puts an added strain on your immune system. But to be beneficial, you need to exercise on a *regular basis*. Organize a routine of exercises or sports that you enjoy and stick with it. Your goal should be to exercise daily, or at least three times a week. If you don't have an exercise routine already, you'll be amazed at the difference it makes in your overall well-being.

WHAT ARE NODES?

Just about every singer at any level has heard of **nodes,** but doesn't always know exactly what they are and what causes them. Nodes are tiny hardened spots that form on the edges of the vocal cords (see Illustration #30.1). They result from continuous vocal abuse. The misuse can be speech or singing related.

Don't worry too much about nodes. The voice can withstand great use, even weather the demands of a heavy performance schedule, when protective measures are taken to maintain vocal health and proper techniques are used when speaking and singing. As an intricate mechanism, there's a limit to how much the voice can take.

ILLUSTRATION #30.1 - Nodes on the Vocal Cords (as seen from above)

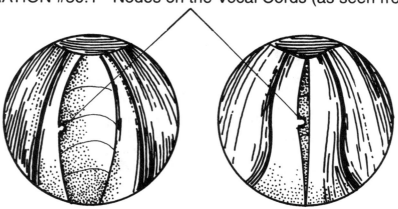

Watch For The Early Warning Signs!

If you feel any of the warning signs of vocal abuse are evident, see a specialist right away. The early warning signs for nodes are:

1) Sudden discomfort or irregular results when initiating tones.

2) Hoarseness or general discomfort after brief periods of talking or singing.

3) Unusual graininess of the speech tone quality.

4) An unintentional breathiness that won't go away.

5) Pitch problems characterized by sudden uncontrollable wavering.

Friedrich S. Brodnitz, in his book, <u>Keep Your Voice Healthy,</u> states "The only effective way of dealing with nodes is to group the treatment around a radical correction of all mistakes in the use of the voice. All other measures have to be subordinated to the task of removing the strain that produced the nodes." If you sing correctly, you should never have a problem with nodes.

A CAUTION TO ALL SINGERS

It's extremely important for singers of all styles, but particularly pop and rock singers, to be aware of correct vocal practices. *Ignorance of good technique can set the stage for permanent vocal damage.*

Unfortunately, the contemporary music scene has created a new breed of singer who is besieged with the tremendous demands placed on his or her vocal resources. More often than not, singers will be asked to perform music that is too demanding for their current abilities or to use the popular "gritty" tone. Listeners often interpret this raspy quality as highly emotional and expressive. Not surprisingly, it's become commonplace in commercials, recordings and concerts and is often seen as the most desirable quality a contemporary singer can attain.

For some singers, this gritty vocal tone does come naturally. They can sing for hours this way and not feel any discomfort. Too many singers, however, desperate to acquire this tone quality, will do just about anything to achieve it, even if it means seriously endangering their vocal well-being.

SING FOR THE MOMENT, AND FOR THE FUTURE

As a result of this attitude, there is a tremendous epidemic of vocal abuse, causing nodes and general vocal impairment. This is occurring on a scale never before witnessed by voice teachers and throat specialists. Young singers and professionals are developing nodes on the vocal cords at an alarming rate. At best, these singers require lengthy vocal rest, and, at worst, serious surgery.

As a contemporary singer, deserving of a long career uninterrupted by vocal disorders, you must jealously guard your vocal resources. Remind those who encourage you to sing too loud, yell, or get that gritty "rock" sound (if it doesn't come naturally to you) that you can't go down to the local music store and simply buy a new pair of cords when yours give out.

Week after week, reports come in about another famous artist whose career is jeopardized due to mishandling of their vocal resources. Voice students as well as professionals should learn from their misfortune. *Be careful with your instrument.* Practice the Secrets of Singing until the techniques are solidly in place. Let your voice develop gradually. The mental and physical shock of having to go through a bout of vocal impairment such as nodes can be extremely traumatic in the early years of a budding career.

Remember, your voice can last you a lifetime. The golden years of singing should be between the ages of thirty five and fifty five. Will you have a voice then? There's an excellent chance that you will if you take your vocal health seriously.

CHAPTER 31
QUESTIONS & ANSWERS

"A moment's insight is sometimes worth a life's experience."

Oliver Wendell Holmes

Q - Should I pull up my soft palate when I sing?

A - Yes, in a manner of speaking. The soft palate or velum, as it's officially called, should be *gently* lifted, as in the very beginning of a yawn. Anything more than this will stiffen the muscles in the back of the throat, and cause your tone to become too brittle.

Q - Should I aim my voice into my nose?

A - No. The voice certainly does have, as one of its characteristics, a bit of nasality. However, putting the voice forward and *in* the nose directs the air column away from the mouth, *the voice's most potent resonator.* As Manuel Garcia aptly said in his <u>Hints on Singing</u>, "the nose is in the voice but, the voice should not be in the nose." After the initiation of tone deep in the throat, fill the mouth with vowels, then lift the voice *behind, above, and around* the nose. Sing *through* the nose rather than *in* the nose.

Q - Will singing be improved if I push for support with my diaphragm?

A - Again, it's a matter of degree. You don't push with the diaphragm when yelling in excitable emotional states, such as anger or joy. Instead, you let out the intensity contained within you, which gives release to the air and energy as well. The diaphragm governs inhalation and together with the rib muscles manages the power (or air) generated by the lower support muscles.

Q - I've been told to press down on my larynx (voice box) to achieve a bigger, deeper sound. Is that O.K.?

A - Grab your coat, don't leave any money on the piano and run for the door. This is the advice of a voice butcher, not a voice teacher. Any type of external bullying of the vocal mechanism can only get you in trouble. The most effective vocal instruction deals first of all with training the mind and then works on balancing vocal elements *below and above but not in the throat.*

Q - Does the attack or beginning of my singing of a note start in the head or the throat?

A - First of all, professional singers don't attack notes, they initiate them gently. Tone begins at the vocal cords (which cause the air to vibrate at a certain frequency), swells in the mouth and throat, and then is enhanced by sympathetic resonance in the head resonators.

Q - Are vocal exercises a waste of time?

A - No. A short carefully constructed, regularly rehearsed group of exercises helps keep the voice toned, flexible and well coordinated. Is a pitcher wasting time when he "warms up" before the first batter arrives at the plate? Singing is a physical activity that improves with adequate and proper preparation.

Q - Are exercises specifically for breathing helpful?

A - Yes and no. If you're a beginner, breath exercises like those contained in this book can be very helpful in quickly identifying the location of, and building, good breathing habits. Breath exercises can also help maintain your instrument's stamina in a period of relative vocal inactivity. However, if you have good breathing habits and sing all the time, breath exercises aren't necessary.

Q - I'm a low-voiced singer. Is it normal that I don't have any high notes?

A - If you're a baritone (medium-low male voice) for instance, your range will usually be lower than that of a tenor (high-voiced male). But all categories of voice (i.e., soprano, tenor, alto, mezzo-soprano, baritone and bass) should have a full range, which includes low, middle and high notes appropriate for their own range.

Q - What makes for better practice, ascending or descending scales?

A -They're both important and both should be included in your practice plan. Descending vocalises are very good practice for initiation of tone. Ascending scales help to balance top notes with the deeper vocal colors of throat and chest resonance. Ascending and descending scales should be worked together to secure an even scale throughout the range.

Q - Can you open your mouth too much for singing?

A -Definitely. Although the majority of beginning and intermediate level singers don't open their mouths enough, in some cases a singer will open the mouth up too much. This causes a strain on the jaw joint and results in a tone which is usually too breathy. Especially in the low range, the voice requires very little opening of the mouth. The jaw should be *comfortably dropped*, as in the beginning of a yawn, not gaping wide open, as in the most exaggerated stage of the yawn.

Q - Should I take a big breath in preparation for singing high or loud notes?

A - No. Nothing could be less helpful. If you know the guidelines for proper breathing and breath control, you never need more than an appropriate sip of air for even the most demanding vocal situations. As soon as you take a big gulp of air, the voice is put at a disadvantage, with potential for easy singing all but lost.

Q - I've been taught to push a lot of heavy books up with my stomach muscles. Does that mean I've developed strong breathing muscles?

A - No, this is a common fallacy. When you push books up with your stomach muscles, all you're perfecting is a "belly-shove" that has nothing to do with true motions of the breathing muscles when they function correctly in singing. The lower breath support work for singing involves muscles *all around the waist - front, back and sides,* not just up front.

Q - Should I tighten my stomach muscles when I sing or vigorously push them out?

A - No. If you take a comfortable and low breath, as you sing, the muscles in and around your stomach will press inwards to the proper degree all by themselves. Attempting to sing with the stomach tight or pulled in only results in a constricted throat (and the appearance of being very stiff and uncomfortable onstage).

Q - Why do I have so much trouble with the OO and EE vowels? Are they harder than the others, such as AH or EH?

A - Yes, OO and EE are a bit tricky in the beginning. But they do relax and eventually, with proper guidance and practice, feel as easy to produce as all the other vowels. As you sing higher in the voice, modify OO with a hint of OH as you keep your jaw comfortably down. Give EE the feel of a slight yawn. If you practice these vowels they'll soon shape up.

Q - Should my chest be as high as possible when I sing?

A - Let's just say it should be comfortably high with the weight of your rib cage, shoulders, neck and head off of the lower breathing muscles and diaphragm. However, don't overdo it and get into some sort of military, stock-straight, artificially pulled-up position. This will only add tension to the instrument.

Q - Should I sing very loudly to "substantially build-up" my voice when practicing?

A - No. *Medium loud* practicing will work wonders if you're practicing correctly with good breath, focus, pathway and anchoring habits in place (that is, in your mind and muscles). *In singing, pain never equals gain!*

Q - Should I bow my head down or lift my head up to accommodate high note or low notes?

A - No. Leave the head alone. It's best to keep the line of the jaw parallel with the floor.

Q - Where should I place my voice? I've had one teacher tell me to sing out the back of my head and another says to place my tone right on my forehead between my eyes.

A - These are simplistic solutions to a very complex question. The voice should never be placed or driven into any one spot of the singer's anatomy. Rather, it partakes of all of the various resonant parts of the instrument. Focusing attention on each of the resonators in turn, such as head, mouth, chest, back of the throat, or teeth can be beneficial, but eventually, you must sing with all of the vibrant parts of the instrument actively and simultaneously involved.

Q - Will it help my singing to flatten or "groove" my tongue?

A - Yes, if it happens gently. The tongue should be flat on the bottom of the mouth, lying much like a rug on the floor with its tip just barely resting up against the back of your bottom teeth. This position is, of course, not possible when singing through words and consonants; but it is very possible when singing exercises on vowels only or holding a note on a vowel in a song. The slight yawn position used in singing encourages the tongue to maintain the correct position.

Q - Is it helpful to maintain a smiling mouth position when singing?

A - No. An artificial smile looks ridiculous when singing serious or dramatic songs. The focus of the voice is also impaired, causing the singer to push too much air in an effort to make up for lost resonance. However, an inner or unseen smile is helpful when performed correctly. See Chapter 4: "Elevating the Voice" for details.

Q - Is imitating famous singers' voices a good way to learn how to sing?

A. Not really. In fact, your chief job is to find your own individual sound. Imitation of another's voice impedes progress. Why? Because in copying the sound of someone else's voice, you'll lose your own quality and tone, and therefore force your voice to function in ways that are unnatural to you. *The result is total confusion at best; ruin, both physically and artistically, at worst.*

As a student, you may want to imitate the sound of a friend who sings well or the method used by an admired famous singer, but don't try to duplicate *exactly* the other individual's unique sound or quality. You may go so far as to imitate the style, color or expression of another, but *never the actual voice.* The exception here is the singer in a "cover" band, whose job it is to mimic the style and sound of famous recording artists. This is best left to singers who have already defined their own sound and can return to it at will.

Q - Should I avoid milk, cheese and other dairy products before singing?

A - This is a very individual question. If you're allergic to dairy products, the answer is yes. If you're not, the answer is no. Singers with a strong, well-rehearsed technique can eat and drink almost anything without any ill effects to their singing (with the exception of alcoholic beverages - see the chapter on Vocal Maintenance). For non-allergic people, milk may give you a temporary excess of phlegm in the throat. But, it's just a minor inconvenience, and when your technique kicks in, means nothing at all.

CHAPTER 32

TROUBLESHOOTING GUIDE

*"Seek to guide your own voice merely by sensation,
not by listening to it."*

Grace Levinson
The Singing Artist

BREATHWORK AND FRAMEWORK

It helps to break down the study of what interferes with the consistency of an ideal tone into two categories. These are **breathwork** and **framework**.

Framework describes all of the component parts from the vocal cords up that constitute good positioning of the head, jaw, neck, tongue, lips, as well as how we deal with the pathway, focus, vowels and consonants.

Breathwork covers all aspects of breathing air in and letting air out, and the delicate process of the initiation of tone. Just like a well-built house, a well sung line is based on a strong foundation of controlled support and framed in a physical environment that is perfectly relaxed and balanced to support long chains of well-formed vowels and consonants.

Dividing up the components of tone in this way is helpful in that when singing, you can begin to analyze the specific faults that foil your attempts to make beautiful connected lines.

CONSTRUCTIVE CRITICISM, PLEASE!

It's important to apply these two general categories to gain the ability to critique yourself constructively. One problem that plagues many singers occurs as they listen to themselves while singing and instantaneously assign a rating to how they're doing. After singing three lines of a song, they're already assigning a grade somewhere between "not as good as my friend sings" and "just plain awful." There's not much gained by this type of self criticism. Nothing changes except your opinion of your own singing, which goes down the drain.

If, however, you get in the habit of taping yourself singing (in other words, reserving all criticism until after you're done) and listening to the playback, you'll have created a much better climate for study and improvement. Singing and critiquing simultaneously is a futile enterprise. Try to get in the habit of singing with 100% of your efforts put towards producing your ideal sound and then critique yourself via a tape recorder afterwards.

Don't set your talent against itself - one part singing versus one part critic.

ANALYZING THE RESULTS

While giving your vocal efforts the undivided attention they deserve, take any of your now familiar exercises or a favorite song and sing while recording your efforts. After the singing is over, play back your taped results and analyze them as to where the problems occur that disturb the even flow of your vocal line.

If the tone quality is weak, wavering, blasting or inconsistent, you can bet your breathwork controls, those discussed at length in the initial sections of this book need to be stronger. On the other hand, if your tones are nasal, thin, raspy, throaty, or seem to bump along from one consonant to the next, you can bet framework features are to blame.

The beauty of this system of practicing and then analyzing, is that if you do it enough, what emerges is a pattern that clearly points out where you need to expend the energy of your practice hours. Some of you will undoubtedly feel that time after time your problems are framework based. Another group of you will find that time after time again, breathwork problems are at the root of your vocal ills.

TRUST YOURSELF

Go with your intuition here. What you feel is the problem, more than likely, is the problem. Work on whatever in the Troubleshooting Guide seems to speak of your particular vocal flaw until the unwanted quality goes away. Re-read whatever chapter in this book relates to the problems consistently indicated by the following guide.

As the next blemish to your consistently well-sung line shows itself, identify it as related to framework or breathwork and make your best assumption as to which specific vocal fault it is. Then go to work on fixing this problem. In this way, you're developing a sense of vocal independence so you'll be able to stand on your own two feet as a professional vocalist.

PROBLEM	EFFECT	LIKELY CAUSE(S)		REMEDY
		Framework	*Breathwork*	
1) Throaty Tone	Tight, brittle, hard quality. Tone doesn't "float."	• No pathway concept in use • Back of throat too open • Rigid jaw/neck • Tone is not focused	• Using too much air • Storing air too high in the chest • Shoulders lifted • Body not relaxed	• Touch tip of tongue to the back of the bottom teeth. • Add inner smile sensation • Add mask resonance (aim through hole in the wall) • Breathe lower (360° around belt level). • Relax neck, jaw, shoulders.
2) Tight Jaw	Not enough space between the molars; teeth clenched together. Overall sound is small. Very little resonance (carrying power).	• Mouth position is not oval • Overarticulation • Jaw not relaxed	Too much air forced into the cords	• Relax tongue and soft palate. • Use a mirror to check mouth position, making sure the jaw is down and oval. • Sing songs and exercises on AH only. When jaw relaxes, re-introduce words and consonants. • *Don't push*; let your voice flow out.
3) Nasal Tone	When a voice seems caught or overly influenced by the nose.	• Mouth too closed • Placing the voice *in* the nose • Tongue too far up or back		• Practice exercises and songs with mirror. Opening mouth and adding a bit of a yawn sensation in throat will balance nasality. Sing around, above and *through* the nose, but not *in* the nose. • Anchor/Double-Anchor-tone

PROBLEM	EFFECT	LIKELY CAUSE(S) Framework	Breathwork	REMEDY
4) Singing Flat	When the voice sounds out of tune. Flat tones occur when the melody as sung falls below the pitch of accompanying instruments, tapes or other singers.	• Throat constricted • Voice focused too low • No lift-ups • Emotional energy lacking • Vowels modified (darkened) too much or too low in range	• Not enough breath flow • Abdomen held rigidly • On modified (covered) vowels, not enough breath support • Lazy posture habits	Use inner smile. Aim for letting the voice pole-vault up the pathway. Add support until in tune. Press, don't push air to the cords. Sing from above and behind, down to any high note. Stand or sit comfortably upright. Energize yourself! Open vowels in low/mid range.
5) Singing Sharp	Voice sounds out of tune. Sharp tones occur when the voice rises too high and actually lies above the pitch of the accompanying instruments, tapes or other singers.	• Voice pushed or aimed out of top of head • Tight jaw • Mouth too closed	• Air pushed or aimed into cords • Too much body tension • Too much air forced into vocal cords	Relax entire body before singing. Focus gently, don't "drive" voice into place. Use smallest amount of air that gets the job done (the "indispensable minimum"). Generally "aim" voice along pathway to insure resonance everywhere. Drop jaw.
6) Attacking the first note of phrases (known as the glottal attack).	Bumping into the first note of a phrase after taking a breath. Shuts down the throat.	• Jaw not down • Throat closed as singing begins	Air shoved into cords all at once.	To avoid shocking the cords, add the half "h." Once throat opens in the breath, keep it slightly yawned as you initiate tone. Use your diaphragm to resist the breath support muscles. Start controlling the air as soon as inhalation is complete, and before the initiation of tone.

PROBLEM	EFFECT	LIKELY CAUSE(S)		REMEDY
		Framework	*Breathwork*	
7) Sliding from note to note.	Vocal line includes sounds like a child's slide whistle, rather than singerly phrasing. The voice is dragged up or slurred down from note to note. Voice sounds limp and weak.	• No yawned position for roof of mouth and tongue • Focus not set	• General weakness of breath muscles • Lazy speech patterns carried over into song	Practice Controlled Release and Pressure Release exercises. Find oval mouth position. Work on focus and add the beginning of a yawn to tone production. Add clear concept of reverse megaphone to shore up mental imagery.
8) Breathy Tone	Voice sounds too "airy," as if too much air is escaping along with tone.	Focus not achieved.	Too much air is being used.	Aim voice (mentally and gently) through the hole in the wall, after leading it up and over the pathway. Exercise breath control. Strengthen overall body tone and lower breathing muscles in particular.
9) Cracking Tone (Dull, colorless tone)	The voice seems to lurch or bump from one quality to another mid-phrase.	• Tongue position too varied • Jaw joints too closed and tense • Slow, lazy consonants that are too big • Trying too hard to manipulate head and chest resonance manually.	Sudden release of excessive air	• Keep tongue touching the back of the bottom teeth • Relax jaw joints. • Keep throat in yawn position (beginning of yawn only). • Make consonants light, crisp and fast. • Keep air flow steady • Practice Messa di Voce. • If persistent, check for nodes. • Strengthen overall body tone and the diaphragm in particular.

PROBLEM	EFFECT	LIKELY CAUSE(S) Framework	Breathwork	REMEDY
10) Lack of Ring	Voice sounds dull or "hooty"	• Angle of reversed megaphone lifting • Tone not following the pathway • Tone is spreading	Air flow too weak	• Mentally picture pathway moving through reverse megaphone. • Imagine the hole-in-the-wall and aim tone through it. • Use oval mouth shape.
11) Vibrato too fast, too slow, or absent	Regarding the characteristic vocal vibration or "throbbing" found in most voices. Unless vocal conditions are favorable, the rate of fluctuation can slow down, speed up, or stop, causing discomfort to performer and audience alike.	All framework factors have to be integrated harmoniously to assure steady, pleasing vibrato.	Pushing air, rather than pressing it.	All vocal factors regarding mouth shape, focus, lift-ups, blend, relaxation, posture, etc. combine together to allow for a natural sounding vibrato if breath control is established. Practice Controlled Release and Pressure Release exercises, along with Messa di Voce.
12) Tense face, "furrowed" brow.	The face, and especially the forehead, wrinkle with lines of tension as singer gives out note of upper range.	Too much "placing" of notes in one spot.	Forcing the maximum amount of air through the cords	• Initiate/begin tones or phrases in all resonant zones at once. • Use the indispensable minimum of air. • Mentally bend top notes back down into the mouth as you gently add air. • Don't aim voice too aggressively anywhere, especially at nose, forehead, or top of head. • Make back of reverse megaphone taller.

319

PROBLEM	EFFECT	LIKELY CAUSE(S)		REMEDY
		Framework	*Breathwork*	
13) Lack of Diction	Words of lyric remain unclear as manner of singing causes consonants and vowels to be indecipherable.	• Tension in tongue • Mouth too closed • Consonants too slow and "back" in the mouth	Not enough breath support	• Relax tongue. • Imagine words created on the tip of tongue at the lips • "Lift up" speech patterns to the heights where singing exists. Get words on the pathway. • Relax jaw joint • Strengthen lower support muscles. • Study Consonant Guides to understand how each consonant is properly formed.

PART SIX:
APPENDICES 1-5
THE ANATOMY OF SINGING

APPENDIX 1:
THE BREATHING SYSTEM

"Basically, one does not learn to breathe correctly - one only relearns the natural breathing that was unconscious in childhood."

Astrid Varnay

THE BREATHING SYSTEM

If you've read through the book on the fast track and practiced the breathing exercises, you already know how powerful the effects of a strong, controlled breathing system are. The anatomical information in this section will fine-tune your breathing by allowing you to visualize what's actually happening when you take a breath.

If you're reading this information before doing the breathing exercises, you'll have greater insight into how the breath support muscles and the diaphragm coordinate to provide the foundation for singing. Since singing begins in your mind, it's essential that you have a clear picture of how your instrument works. Understanding the mechanics of the breathing system is an important step in "building" your instrument.

The Breath Support Muscles

The abdominal muscles, lower ribs (intercostal muscles), and lower back muscles work with the diaphragm to provide support to the entire breathing system. These muscles are the ones you feel when you do sit-ups or leg raises (see Illustration #A1.1 a b & c).

ILLUSTRATIONS #A1.1 (a)(b)(c) -
The Breath Support Muscle Group

a) Back　　　　　　b) Side　　　　　　c) Front

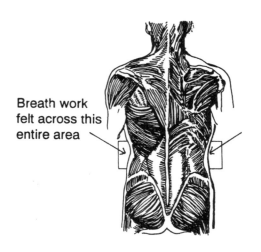

Breath work felt across this entire area

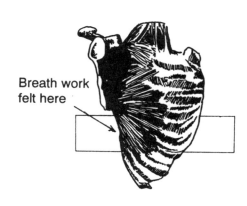

Breath work felt here

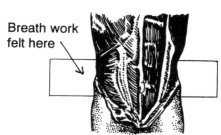

Breath work felt here

Right before you take in air, the breath support muscles (front, sides, and back) must relax, allowing the intestinal mass to relax also, so that the diaphragm can descend. The stomach should never be rigid when bringing air into the lungs. Even when singing, *the stomach should be flexibly firm, but with give in it.*

The considerable lower strength added to the singing instrument by the breath support muscles is as important as the diaphragm itself. Greater endurance, singing high notes with ease, and holding notes for a long time and comfortably are the direct results of effective use of these powerful muscles.

The Diaphragm

The diaphragm is a large muscle which divides the abdomen into two parts, upper and lower. At rest, it forms an arch which is rather high in the abdominal cavity. A split second before you take a breath, it descends and flattens out (see Illustration A1.2 a & b).

ILLUSTRATION #A1.2 (a) (b) - The Diaphragm

a) At Rest   b) Positioned for Inhalation and Control

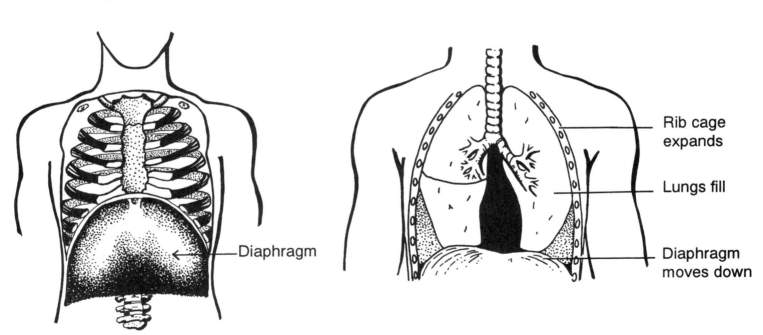

When the diaphragm descends, it leaves empty space in the abdomen, which in turn creates a partial vacuum or low pressure area in and around the lungs. Air outside your body, which is at normal air pressure, rushes into the lungs to stabilize the pressure and to fill the space left by the lowered diaphragm (see Illustration #A1.3).

ILLUSTRATION #A1.3 -
Movement of Diaphragm (Inhalation & Exhalation)

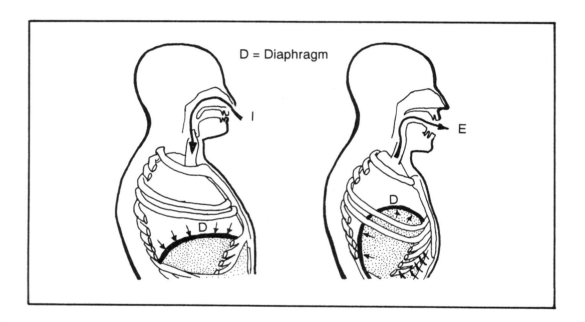

The significance of the diaphragm as a muscle of breath support is over-emphasized by most singing schools and teachers. The diaphragm is, however, undeniably the most important muscle of *inhalation* and contributes in no small way to breath control. The lowering of the diaphragm makes room for the lungs to inflate. And how slowly the muscle returns to its place of rest is largely the measure of breath control.

A trained **diaphragm** becomes coordinated with the support muscles to allow for faster, deeper, and more controlled inhalation. This contributes to the elimination of gulping or panic breaths which are common among inexperienced singers.

When singing, the diaphragm and lower rib muscles gently but persuasively resist the rising movement of the lower support muscles. After inhaling, the lower rib/diaphragm duo mimics the feeling of "a woman in labor, giving birth...you push like that" (down with the diaphragm and out with the lower rib muscles), as Luciano Pavarotti states in Jerome Hines book *Great Singers on Great Singing*.

Without this restraint on the breath flow, too much air will strike the cords and tone quality will be lessened or distorted. Whether pressing air up with the lower support muscles or resisting down and out with the control muscles, never flex any muscle to the point of rigidity, but only flexible firmness.

James Terry Lawson, M.D. in his clear-cut, concise book *Full Throated Ease* perfectly illustrates and describes the sensation of breath control this way: (see Illustration #A1.4). "The sense of 'stretch' or 'pull' between the diaphragm and the palate is a valuable aid to good resonance and good tone-placing. It will come to you in time. It will feel almost as if the vocal cords were attached to an elastic {band} stretched from the palate to the diaphragm. When you achieve just right the tension in the elastic, the voice-box is suspended just the right distance from the palate to produce a good resonant sound:

ILLUSTRATION #A1.4 - Coordination of Support Muscles and Diaphragm

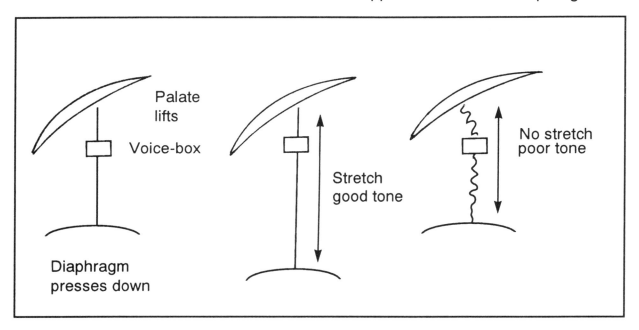

The palate is fixed 'high'. The diaphragm held tight below. The box rides free on the elastic between the two. The throat is open and relaxed."

THE LUNGS

The lungs inflate and deflate during breathing or singing, acting as bellows for the vocal system. They have no muscular strength and even their shape is determined by the movements of the ribs, diaphragm and the amount of air contained within.

Vital Capacity vs. Reserve Air

When you take a breath, you're always taking in more air than you think. In fact, you *always* have more air in your lungs than it feels like you have. *When it seems like you're out of air, you're not!* There's always a certain amount of air - known as *residual or reserve air* - left over. That's because the capacity of your lungs (the actual amount of air that the lungs can hold) is never completely emptied during normal exhalation or singing (see Illustration #A1.5). In the illustration, your vital capacity is notated by the darkened region, while your safety net –the reserve air – is indicated by the light area.

ILLUSTRATION #A1.5 - Lungs, Vital/Reserve Capacity

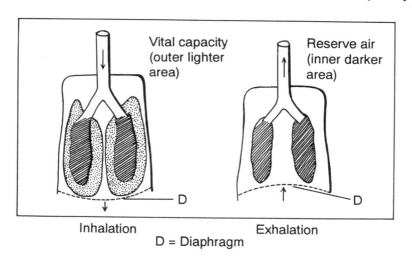

To get an idea of how much reserve air is left after you exhale, try the following experiment. Fill your lungs completely and then exhale until you feel that your lungs are nearly empty. Now, *before taking another breath*, sing a few phrases of your favorite song, pressing the last little bit of air into service as your singing breath. What happens? You find that you <u>can</u> squeeze even more air out of the lungs! It may have *seemed* that you had drained the lungs of air in the first place, but there's always some air left over.

Have you ever panicked at the end of a long phrase or when sustaining a note because you felt like you'd used up all of your air? Just knowing that there's more air stored than it seems will help ease this feeling.

The key is in developing your diaphragm and support muscles. If these muscles are strong and controlled, they'll be able to squeeze a portion of the reserve air out of the lungs, providing plenty of air to sing any phrase. Successful singers use this secret to sustain the long phrases and notes that never fail to impress an audience. They also know that singing requires a surprisingly small amount of air!

The Trachea or "Windpipe"

Air travels in and out of the lungs through the trachea, more commonly called the windpipe. The windpipe is a rather inflexible tube made up of rings of soft bone or cartilage, much like the hose of a canister vacuum cleaner (see Illustration #A1.6 below).

ILLUSTRATION #A1.6 - The Trachea or "Windpipe"

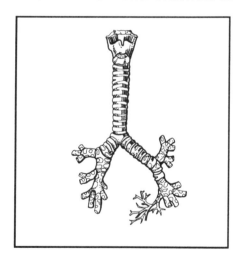

Muscles toward the rear of the trachea automatically expand the diameter of the windpipe during exhalation and relax on inhalation. That's why some teachers suggest that you imagine that you're still inhaling when you sing. It's good advice —anything you can do to keep the instrument open is beneficial.

APPENDIX 2:
THE VOCAL APPARATUS

"Nothing is so strong as gentleness; nothing so gentle as real strength."

St. Francis de Sales

One of the most misunderstood aspects of singing is the vocal apparatus, consisting of the larynx and vocal cords. Many singers unknowingly mistreat their voices because they just don't understand how the vocal cords work.

Unless you learn the subtleties of how the vocal cords work, you can easily fall into the trap of concentrating on the throat too much. That's the last thing you want to do! Read through this section carefully; it will help you to avoid some of the troublesome problems singers of all styles encounter.

The Larynx or "Voice Box"

The larynx, or "voice box," consists of a set of bones located in the front of the neck at the top of the windpipe. The voice box encases and protects the vocal cords (see Illustration #A2.1 below).

ILLUSTRATION #A2.1 -
Side View of the Larynx or "Voice Box"

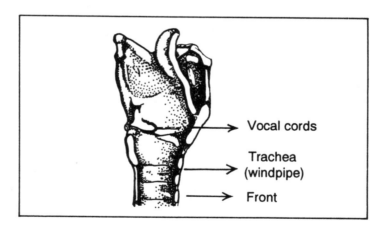

It's important to realize that the voice box is forward in the throat, not in the center or towards the back of the neck. To find your own voice box, feel for the little bulge at the location as indicated in Illustration #A2.2.

ILLUSTRATION #A2.2 - Location of the Voice Box

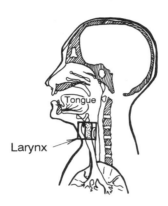

Remember, in singing, what you think is what you get. Study the illustration carefully so you can accurately visualize where the voice box is. If you don't have an accurate picture in your mind of where it's located, your mind will be working against your instrument. Singing with the wrong picture in your mind is like holding a guitar wrong or using the wrong wrist position for keyboard playing; it just won't be right.

THE VOCAL CORDS

Inside the voice box, there's a very important valve which controls the flow of air to and from the lungs. The valve is known by many names, such as: the vocal bands, vocal folds or vocal cords.

ILLUSTRATION #A2.3 - The Vocal Cords and Glottis

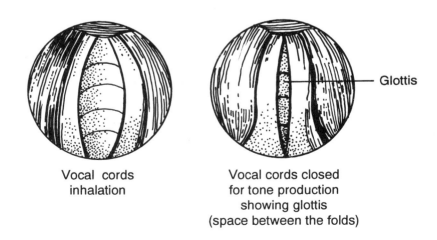

Vocal cords
inhalation

Vocal cords closed
for tone production
showing glottis
(space between the folds)

Though many people think of the vocal cords as being strung vertically, they are actually strung *horizontally* across the voice box (see Illustration #A2.3). There is a space between the two cords known as the **glottis.** As you sing up a scale, the glottis narrows. The higher the note, the narrower the space between the cords. The cords never completely close, though, since if they did, no sound would be able to get through.

Think of the cords as meeting like the two halves of a zipper as you sing higher. After opening for inhalation, they actually "zip" closer together from front to back as you sing higher and higher (Illustration #A2.4). This causes the vibrating parts of the cords to become smaller and smaller.

ILLUSTRATION #A2.4 -
Zipper-like Action of the Cords

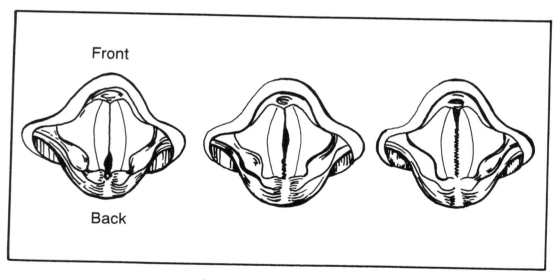

(as seen from above)

The cords function much like the faucet on a sink by preventing or allowing the flow of air. More precisely, the diaphragm and lower support muscles press air up against the cords, and as a result of the increased air flow, the cords come together to resist the passage of air. There are many small muscles in the voice box which help the vocal cords resist the movement of air. The cords don't resist to the point of closing, however, because the air pressure from below overcomes the cords just enough to keep them apart.

In addition to this air pressure from below, an interesting phenomenon occurs as the air moves through the cords: as the air is blown through the glottis, it creates a suction which pulls the cords back together again. This suction is the force that keeps the cords vibrating (opening and closing) at a consistent rate. The cords vibrate at a rate of hundreds, even thousands, of times per second. The rate of the opening and closing of the vocal cords determines pitch. The higher you sing, the faster the vocal cords open and close.

There must be a balance between the pressure from below (from the diaphragm and breath support muscles) and the resistance of the cords. The cords resist to the degree that air is pressed against them from below. If your breathing system is too weak or lacks control, it won't send the right amount of air to the cords: either too little air reaches the cords (and you'll have a weak sound) or too much air will hit the cords, causing them to tighten too much. **Overblowing,** when too much air is moved into the vocal cords, is one of the most common sources of tension and fatigue throughout the throat area.

While the vocal cords are obviously of monumental importance in singing, remember that *the action of the vocal cords is involuntary*. Therefore, other than understanding the basic mechanics of the cords, don't try to "work" on your vocal cords. In fact, the less you think about them, the better your technique will be.

APPENDIX 3:
THE RESONATORS

"I just sing. I don't know what I sound like or who I sound like. I don't know what kind of a singer I am. I just open my mouth and sing."

Sarah Vaughan

The resonation system is what makes your voice unique. Each singer's breathing system is pretty much the same (though individuals will differ in their level of development of control and support); every singer's vocal cords are vibrating at 440 cycles per second when they're singing the A just above middle C on the piano. *But no one has exactly the same set-up in terms of the resonant bones and cavities as you do.*

The size of the lower resonators: larynx (voice box), pharynx (throat), mouth and the chest, will vary from person to person. More importantly, the size and shape of the bones and cavities of the skull known as the "mask" are totally different in every person.

Studying this section, in conjunction with the chapter on blend, will help you understand the details of the resonation system. When you've mastered focus and anchoring, the "sound" of your voice will *emerge* naturally, without forcing it to "become" unique.

THE CHEST

The chest or thoracic cavity is the part of the human body between the neck and the diaphragm, that's partially encased by ribs. As discussed at the beginning of chapter 11, this area is not a true resonator being full of organs etc., but a section of the body that vibrates in sympathy with amplification occurring in the depths of the throat.

However, there are undeniable psychological and technical benefits from singing high tones with their feet, so to speak, firmly planted on the solid ground of the chest. Imagery used to achieve this balanced approach to mixed resonance can be found in chapter 7.

THE LARYNX OR "VOICE BOX"

The larynx or voice box is the first source of tone amplification (see Illustration #A3.1). Not only does it surround and protect the cords, but it also has the characteristics of a good resonator: effective resonators result from a hard casing surrounding a hollow.

ILLUSTRATION #A3.1 - The Voice Box (Several Views Close-Up)

Internal View of Voice Box
Showing Resonation Space

The Bones of the Larynx
(Voice Box)

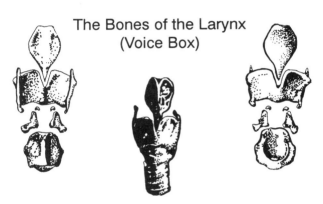

According to Vennard, the widely respected voice specialist, "our most prized resonance may be here [in the voice box itself]." The volume of the tone produced at the vocal cords compared to the volume that comes out of a singer's mouth is analogous to the volume produced by an electric guitar before and after it is amplified.

THE PHARYNX (THROAT)

The pharynx extends from the top of the voice box all the way up to the back of the nasal sinuses. The pharynx is divided into three smaller sections (see Illustration #A3.2): the laryngopharynx (the region of the throat surrounding the larynx), the oropharynx (the back of the mouth), and the nasopharynx (located in the upper throat directly behind the nose).

ILLUSTRATION #A3.2 - The Pharynx

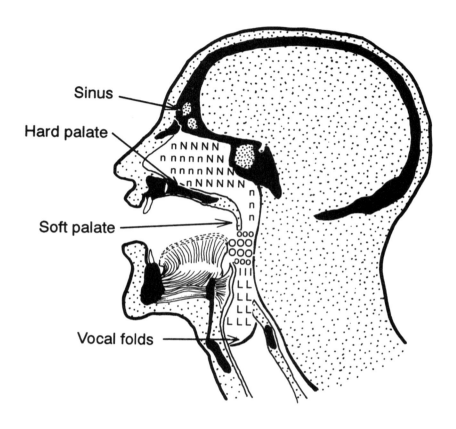

N – Naso-pharynx (behind nose)
O – Oro-pharynx (rear of mouth)
L – Laryngo-pharynx (bottom of throat)

Although authorities on singing often argue about vocal techniques, there is one area of resounding agreement and that is regarding the significance of the "open throat." To achieve maximum and balanced resonance, the three parts of the pharynx *must* work together as a whole. When the throat cavities are open and interconnected, the voice is imbued with mellowness and fullness from the lower regions and brilliance and clarity from the upper regions.

THE MOUTH

The mouth also plays a considerable role in enlarging and enhancing vocal quality. The unique structure of your teeth, lips, jaw and the overall size of your mouth cavity contribute to your own special sound. Ideally, the three parts of the pharynx and the mouth should act as one resonator (see Illustration #A3.3).

ILLUSTRATION #A3.3 - Mouth and Throat (Pharynx) Working Together

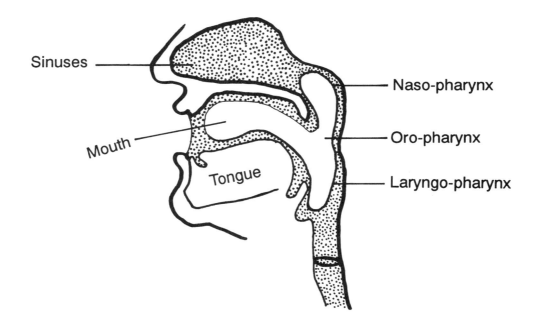

At times, however, they can be split into two if the tongue moves too far back or up in the mouth, creating a barrier in the throat (see Illustration #A3.4 below).

ILLUSTRATION #A3.4 -
Mouth and Throat (Pharynx) Split in Two by Tongue

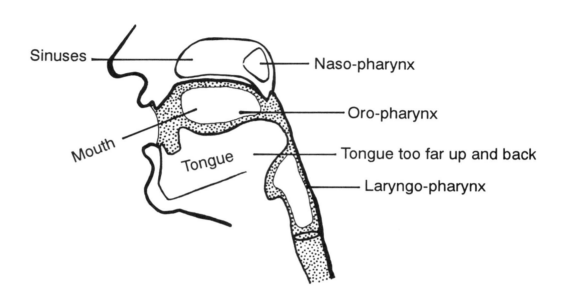

When singing, tone must be shaped into words without the tongue, teeth, or lips restricting the free flow of air (any more than in normal speech). As your vocal work progresses, the mouth will play an ever-increasing role in maintaining your poise as a vocalist. The mouth staying "full" of voice will be an indication of a truly open throat. This is explained in detail in the anchoring section.

THE MASK

Directly above, behind, and beside the nose are the nasal resonators. This area consists of small bones surrounding or accompanied by small cavities called sinuses (see Illustration #A3.5).

ILLUSTRATION #A3.5 - Bones and Cavities of
Nasal Resonators (Directly Behind the Nose)

(Frontal View)

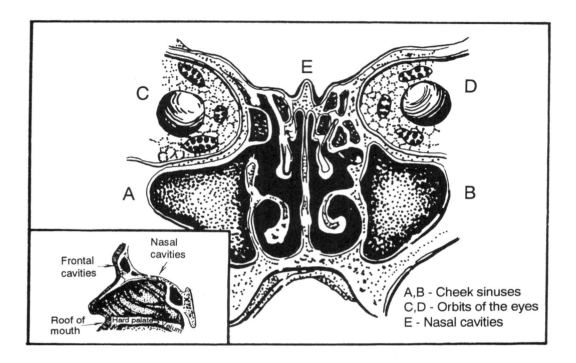

A,B - Cheek sinuses
C,D - Orbits of the eyes
E - Nasal cavities

In addition to the nasal resonators, there are the maxillary bones and cavities located in the cheekbones and the frontal resonators, which are buried in the forehead just beneath and above the eyebrows. Together, these bones and cavities form the powerful resonator known as the "mask." The mask is extremely important in forming the tonal quality of your voice and is discussed at length in the section on focus.

As with all resonating zones, bone and cavities combine to add "ring" or richness and some volume to your tone. Together, they build up the vibration coming from the cords. Illustration #A3.6 below shows how the various resonators of the head are interconnected to enhance the high qualities of the tones you sing. Edge, ring, ping, brilliance, buzz, and focus are all terms used to describe the qualities added to the voice and intensified in the head bones of the mask.

ILLUSTRATION #A3.6 -
Passageways Connecting the Various Head Resonators

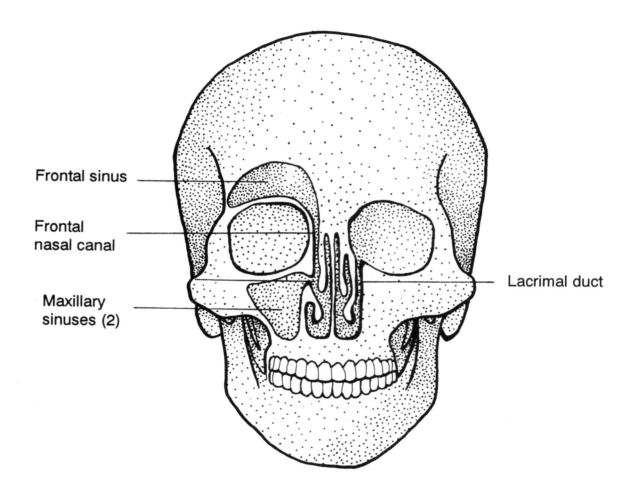

Frontal sinus

Frontal
nasal canal

Maxillary
sinuses (2)

Lacrimal duct

APPENDIX 4:
THE ARTICULATORS

"Do not feel any change take place when you pass from speech to song. Music is not put into words; it pervades them."

Edward Bairstow
Harry Plunket Greene
Singing Learned From Speech

The consonants can be organized for discussion by the part of the speech mechanism directly involved in their production. The following Articulator Chart will give you an opportunity to become familiar with how the mouth parts and consonants work together. It may be helpful to refer to illustration #26.1"The Articulators" in the Consonants chapter as you read through the information below.

THE ARTICULATORS:
HOW CONSONANTS ARE PRODUCED

CONSONANT	ARTICULATOR	HOW CONSONANT IS PRODUCED
T, D, Z	Tongue and Upper Gums, Behind Two Top Front Teeth	The tip of the tongue contacts the front of the hard palate.
S, L, TH	Tongue and Teeth	The tip of the tongue lifts near or contacts the bottom edge of the front top teeth.
R, Y, CH, SH, J	Tongue and Palate	The top and/or sides of the tongue lift up to touch the palate.
K, Q, Hard C (as in cat), Hard G (as in great), NG, X	Tongue and Soft Palate	The back of the tongue moves up to meet the soft palate (velum).

THE ARTICULATORS:
HOW CONSONANTS ARE PRODUCED

CONSONANT	ARTICULATOR	HOW CONSONANT IS PRODUCED
N	Tongue and Upper Gums	Tip of tongue presses against the front of the hard palate, as tone is directed over the roof of the mouth into the head resonators (nasalized).
P, W, B	Lips	The lips participate in the articulation process in two ways: • Press upon each other (with W, the lips barely touch and round together, compressing the air); OR • For P and B, the lips close together, creating a temporary obstruction in the pathway.
V, F	Upper lip and teeth	Top teeth gently press down on or towards bottom lip.
M	Lips	Lips press together as tone is directed over the roof of the mouth into the head resonators (nasalized).

ILLUSTRATION #A4.1 - Articulators

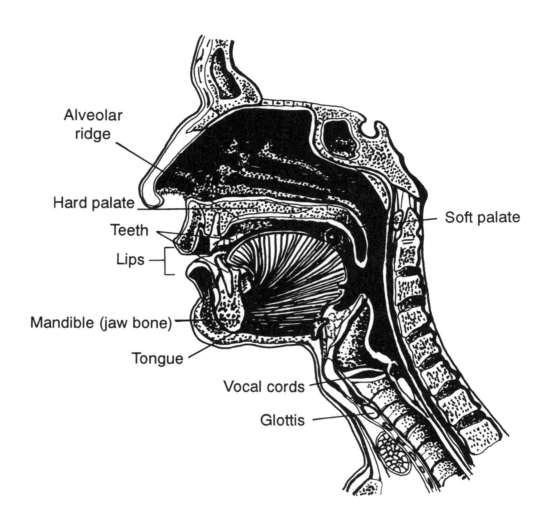

APPENDIX 5: LIST OF EXERCISES

COMMON VOCAL TERMS

"Singing lessons are like body building for your larynx."

Bernadette Peters

Adduct - To close the cords together.

Anchor - To fill the mouth with head and throat/chest resonance resonance.

Approximate - Used to describe the cords coming close together.

Aria - Song, especially an operatic solo.

Arpeggio - Designating a passage in which the voice sounds the note of a chord one after another. Literally, "harp-like" (Italian).

Articulation - Distinct pronunciation. A speech sound, especially a consonant that is formed clearly.

Articulator - The parts of the mouth involved in the creation of sounds or speech (i.e., the mouth, tongue, teeth, and lips).

Attack - The rough onset or beginning of a musical tone at the vocal cords.

Back - Having the resonance in the throat. Opposite: "forward."

Baritone - Average male voice, higher than bass and lower than tenor.

Base - The position of the feet as they relate to and form the base of the vocal instrument.

Bass, Basso - Lowest of the male voices.

Belly Breathing - Breathing by descent of the diaphragm and contraction of the abdominal muscles, in alternation.

Blade of the Tongue - Front flat, part of the tongue.

Blend - To mix qualities of both head <u>and</u> throat/chest resonance to achieve the tone quality desired. By blending correctly, a "crack" or "break" between registers is eliminated.

Blowing - Supplying air as in sounding a wind instrument.

Break - An undesirable change in tone quality when bridging or joining registers. A break commonly occurs when singers blend resonances according to the two or three register systems.

Breast Bone - Bone to which the ribs join in front; the sternum.

Breath Control - Maintenance of breath pressure through resistance provided by the diaphragm and lower ribs.

Breath Flow - Volume of breath expenditure.

Breath Management - Efficient use of air for singing or playing a wind instrument.

Breath Support - The controlled movement of air from the breath support muscle group to the vocal cords.

Breath Support Muscle Group - The group of muscles which provide support to the breathing system. Consists of the abdominal muscles, lower rib (intercostal) muscles, and lower back muscles.

Breathing - Process of taking in breath and expelling it again.

Breathy - A term used to describe a kind of sound in singing that suggests the emission of breath not focused into tone.

Bright - Mask-oriented and well-supported tone.

Brilliance - Tone partaking of head or mask resonance and well-supported.

Catch Breath - A quick or partial breath to renew lung supply.

Chest - Upper part of the trunk.

Chest Resonance - Misnomer applied to a heavy vocal quality arising from the low spaces of the throat along with some sympathetic resonance in the chest cavity.

Clavicle - Bone extending between the shoulder blade and the breast bone; the collar bone.

Clavicular Breathing - Characterized by an improper heaving upward of the chest, alternately raising and lowering the clavicle (collar bone).

Clear - Unmuffled and free from breathiness.

Coloratura Soprano - Highest of the female voices, with considerable range and flexibility above high C.

Compound Vowel - Syllables of words containing two or more vowel sounds spoken or sung in rapid succession.

Consonant - Speech sound, chiefly noise, usually creating momentary obstructions in the airflow.

Consonant Modifications - Adjustments made (in the upper range of the voice only) to lessen the interference of unvoiced consonants on phrasing. Unvoiced consonants are generally modified to their closest voiced counterpart.

Constrictive Vowels - EE and OO, which cause the mouth to move toward a closed position. Special care must be taken when singing EE and OO to keep the throat open and clear.

Controlled Release Exercise - A vocal workout in which a breath is taken, then the air is exhaled very slowly over thirty seconds or more. This helps to locate and develop strength in the breath support muscle group.

Counterbalance - To balance the effects of tones rising in pitch by keeping the jaw, tongue, breath focus and resonance <u>down</u>.

Covered - Singing characterized by a darker or rounded tone quality. Opposite: yelly, strident.

Crack - See "Break."

Dark Timbre - Tone produced with a low larynx and an arched velum. Often used to indicate tone which is lacking in mask resonance or brilliance.

Darkening Vowels - See "Vowel Modifications."

Depressed Larynx - Adjustment produced by pressing the back of the tongue too far down. Usually results in the larynx being lowered too far and causing constriction of tone.

Depth - Tone quality characterized by throat/chest resonance.

Diaphragm - Large dome-shaped muscle that provides a floor for the upper chest, governs inhalation and assists in <u>controlling</u> the flow of air to the cords when singing.

Diction - In singing, clearly enunciating vowels and distinctly articulating consonants.

Diphthong - A complex sound made by gliding continuously from one vowel to another within the same syllable.

Double-Anchor - A method used to stabilize notes sung in the highest range of the voice. Chest resonance is added by degree until the natural brilliance of top notes is balanced with mouth and throat/chest resonance.

Dramatic Soprano - Soprano whose voice is powerful enough for extravagantly emotional roles or songs.

Dramatic Tenor - Tenor whose voice is powerful enough for extravagantly emotional roles or songs.

Dynamics - That aspect of musical expression which pertains to the variation of intensity between soft and loud.

Ear - The whole auditory system which consciously or unconsciously monitors tone production.

Edge - Another term for brilliance or ping in the vocal tone.

Emotion - The feeling of passion which is supported by technique in vocal performance.

Energy - Power to do vocal work.

Enunciation - One of the elements of diction that deals principally with words, their sound, accent and clarity; in singing, especially regarding vowels.

Exercise (vocal) - Work for the sake of attaining proper singing habits.

Exhalation - Expiration; breathing out; in singing, tone production.

Expression - Interpretation, attitude; the revealing of mood, feeling and musical intent in song.

Falsetto - When head resonance is largely divorced from mouth resonance and unsupported.

Floating Tone - A free, soaring vocal quality usually achieved on sustained tones when all singing conditions are optimal.

Floating - Free; well-supported and controlled.

Floating Ribs - Lowest of the bones of the rib cage.

Florid - Vocal music that is ornamental or embellished with many trills and runs.

Flowing - Smoothly produced; free.

Focal Point - See "Focus."

Focus - A term covering the coordination of all the muscular factors and imagery that contribute to the production of an agreeable, free, and ringing voice. Clear; "forward."

Forced - Produced with too much effort of the lower breath support muscles.

Forced Breathing - Breathing, in which too much effort is exerted to inhale and exhale, or too much air is moved to the cords.

Forward - Having resonance of the mask. Opposite: "back."

Glottal Shock - Occurs when the cords strike upon each other.

Glottis - The opening between the vocal cords.

Great Scale - A major scale, two octaves in length. In singing, the Great Scale is especially useful in developing breath control and practicing blend and vowel modifications.

Half-Voice - Vocal tone where head and throat/chest resonance is largely divorced from support.

Hard Palate - Forward part of the roof of the mouth, with bone; distinct from soft palate.

Head Voice/Resonance - A type of light vocal production, often at the upper extreme of a singer's range, distinguished from a similar tone quality which is abundantly supported.

High - "Placed above the roof of the mouth". May also be used in reference to a position of the soft palate advantageous for singing in the upper range. Opposite: "Deep."

High Larynx - Adjustment produced by allowing the larynx to rise as one sings higher. Usually indicates a disability where tone is cut off.

Hole-in-the-Wall - An image used to help singers develop focus or add brilliance to the voice.

Hum - Vocal sound made with closed lips. (For singers, humming also requires keeping the throat open and relaxed by adding the feeling of the beginning of a yawn).

Imagery - Figures of speech to express vocal concepts which are difficult to understand literally.

Imaginary, half, or silent "H" - Beginning a tone with a bit of an "h", which allows a very small puff of air to prepare the cords for a smooth initiation of tone.

Indispensable Minimum - Term coined by E. Herbert Caesari to describe the amount of air that should be used at all times when singing - the smallest amount of air absolutely required to sing a phrase or passage.

Intensity - Amount of air or volume of a note or phrase.

Intercostals - The muscles between the ribs.

Key-note - The first note of a scale (or exercise), upon which the series of notes is based.

Larynx - The "voice box"; the vocal organ, which is located at the top of the trachea and base of the tongue which contains the vocal cords.

Legato - From legare, meaning "to bind" or "tie", and referring to a smooth (bound) passage from one note to the other.

Line - An essential of musical artistry, implying smooth connection between consecutive notes and consistency of vocal quality.

Lower Breath Support Muscles - All of the abdominal parts that combine to exert effort up onto the lungs resulting in the release of air into the vocal cords and upper resonators.

Lung - Each of two breathing organs in the chest.

Lyric - A poem especially suited to vocal performance.

Lyric Soprano - A female singer with a medium weight, flexible voice, but not as high as coloratura soprano or as heavy as a dramatic soprano.

Lyric Tenor - A male singer with a medium weight, flexible voice.

Mandible - Lower jaw.

Mask - The bones and cavities of the cheekbones, forehead, and vicinity of the nose which are part of the voice's natural amplification and resonation system. Tones focused in the mask are said to have "brilliance," or "ping."

Mask Brilliance - Forward placement.

Maxillary Sinus - Sinus buried in the cheekbones on each side.

Melisma - Another term for ornamentation or embellishment. As commonly used now, it refers to ornamentation of an especially elaborate or flowery type. It may be applied most aptly to the type of improvised runs widely practiced by gospel singers or those influenced by such music.

Mellow - Amplification characterized by having strength in the lower regions of resonance. "Rich", "deep", "full."

Melody - Pleasing and rhythmical series of tone.

Messa di Voce - Classic Italian exercise consisting of a prolonged crescendo and decrescendo (or vice versa) on a sustained tone.

Mezza Voce - half-voice.

Mezzo-soprano - Average range female voice, higher than contralto and lower than soprano. May sometimes reach soprano range but with deeper tone quality.

Mouth - Cavity bounded by the lips, cheeks, tongue, and palate. Also known as the oral cavity.

Muscle - Organ which by contraction produces bodily movement.

Nasal Consonant - Voiced tone that is directed through the nose by the articulators. "N" or "M."

Nasality - Quality produced by using the nose as a resonator.

Node, Nodule - Knot or tumor produced by friction between vocal cords. Common among singers who abuse their voices.

One Register System - A system used for blending head and throat/chest resonance. In this method, each note is considered its own register, that is, each note has a specific setting of the vocal cords, mouth position, etc. This way of thinking helps eliminate the break or crack that commonly occurs when trying to manually adjust registers, as in the two or three register systems.

Open - Produced with pure vowels without modification.

Open Throat - Condition agreed upon by most voice teachers as desirable for resonance. Large pharynx.

Opera - Large musical work in which drama and music are combined and soloists both sing and act.

Oral Cavity - Mouth.

Ornament - Notes not in the written music, added to enhance the music. Embellishment.

Overblowing - The condition of air moving to the cords with too much pressure. A result of poor breath control and/or tension.

Passaggio - Refers to the area in the vocal range where the voice seems to "pass" from one quality to another.

Pathway - The literal route that air takes from the vocal cords to outside of the mouth. Also used as an imagined image to give height and roundness to vocal tone.

Penultimate - Literally "next to last." Usually refers to the notes preceding a jump to a top note. These notes serve as "set-up" notes for the top note.

Pharynx - Resonant areas of the throat above the larynx, towards the rear of the mouth, and behind the nasal cavities.

Phrasing - Division of a piece of music into small units for some artistic or technical purpose; especially, into units which can be sung on one breath.

Piercing - Shrill; tight; disturbing to the listener.

Pinched Tone - Constricted throat passage, often with the cords overtightened due to usage of too much air.

Ping - An expression for the characteristic ring of well-sung high notes. Same as "focus;" "edge."

Placement - Figure of speech describing the sensation that tones of differing quality are in different parts of the body.

Point of View (P.O.V.) - An image used to achieve counterbalancing in the upper range. "High" notes, when approached from the Point of View of above and behind, become as manageable as all other notes.

Posture - Position of the body.

Power - Energy; intensity.

Practice - Vocal exercise for the purpose of attaining excellence in technique and beauty of tone.

Pressure - Usually refers to breath pressure, the force of breath energy against vocal cord resistance. A balance of these two forces is ideal.

Pressure Release Exercise - A breath work-out which helps singers locate the source of breath support. Practiced regularly, this exercise builds breath support.

Reaching For The Tone - Tensing the throat by extending the head and jaw upward and forward while allowing the larynx to rise with the pitch. This usually gives the audience the impression that the singer is uncomfortable singing in the upper range. The opposite of counterbalancing.

Register - A term used to designate a certain area of the vocal range, or compass.

Reserve Breath - That part of the lung capacity which is not used in normal breathing.

Residual Breath - Air remaining in the lungs after forced exhalation, which cannot be voluntarily expired, but which escapes when the lungs are collapsed.

Reversed Megaphone - A mental construct which helps to focus the voice (the large end of the megaphone being visualized in the back of the throat; the small end in front of the lips).

Rib Breathing - Breathing by moving the ribs; costal breathing.

Rich - A characteristic of tone when head and throat/chest resonance are anchored together in the mouth.

Riff - An embellishment consisting of an improvised series of notes.

Ring - A quality produced when the vocal cords vibrate freely and tone is amplified simultaneously in the bones and cavities of the larynx, pharynx, mouth, head and chest.

Root of the Tongue - Rear portion of the tongue.

Scale - A graduated series of tones ascending or descending according to a distinctive interval pattern determined by musical convention.

Scat - A term given to a kind of singing in which the singer improvises on syllables of no textual significance.

Shoulder Breathing - Inhalation characterized by excessive lifting of the shoulders and chest. Allows no control over exhalation and should be replaced by low, simultaneous usage of the lower ribs, diaphragm and breath support muscle group.

Simultaneity - The component parts of vocal technique executed all together and at exactly the same time.

Skull - Bony framework of the head.

Slur - A kind of exaggerated legato, in which the note of destination is approached in a sliding manner, usually from below, as opposed to a "clean" passage from one note to the next. Can indicate weak breathing muscles.

Soft Palate - Also called the "velum"; the rearmost extension of the palatal arch (roof of the mouth) which is without cartilaginous or bony inner structure.

Soprano - Highest of the female voices.

Spread - An unfocused vowel characterized by a breathy quality, often caused by mouth position that's too wide.

Staccato - From "staccare " (Italian) meaning "to detach," and referring to notes sung lightly and then quickly released.

Stage Presence - The total impression of a singer's appearance and actions to an audience.

Stage Fright - Any discomfort, anxiety, or nervousness based on the presence of an audience.

Sternocleidomastoid - A muscle on each side of the neck attaching to the skull behind the ears and extending down to the breastbone.

Sternum - Bone to which the ribs join in front; the breastbone.

Stiffness - Any rigidity of the breathing muscles or throat, producing a strained vocal quality.

Strained - Forced.

Straight Tone - A tone without the natural vibrato which is characteristic of free production.

Strident - Loud and harsh; shrill.

Supported - Having adequate breath pressure.

Sympathetic Resonance, Vibration - A sensation occurring when vibration originating at the vocal cords excites a secondary amplifier such as the chest or sinus cavities.

Telegraph - Lifting up or tensing part of the body in a manner obvious to the audience while singing difficult passages or "high" notes.

Tenor - Highest of the male voices.

Tense, Tight Throat - A constricted pathway.

Tessitura - Pitch level in which most of the notes of a given part lie. If this is high, that which is sung is said to have a "high tessitura."

Text - Words, as of a song.

Three Register System - A system of blending vocal colors which breaks the voice into three parts: high, middle, and low.

Throat - Pharynx. Entire region of the neck which contains, among other things, the passageway of air into and out of the lungs. An area essential to the amplification of vocal tone.

Throaty - Tone which is "swallowed," or "dark."

Tight - Vocal tone produced with too much tension, often with a constricted throat. Opposite: free, floating.

Timbre - The characteristic quality of vocal sound that distinguishes one voice from another. It is determined by each instrument's distinctive combination of harmonics.

Trachea - Cartilaginous tube through which air passes in and out of the lungs; the windpipe.

Trapezius - Large, flat, triangular muscle joining the shoulder blade and collarbone to the spine, and running up to the back of the skull.

Tremolo - A kind of vocal movement characterized by tone which is pulsating or oscillating too fast (as in a vibrato that's too rapid).

Triphthong - A combination of three vowel sounds in a single syllable.

Two Register System - A commonly taught system of blending vocal colors which separates the voice into two parts: high and low.

Unvoiced Consonants - A speech sound that obstructs the flow of air, and there is no attendant vibration of cord.

Velum - Soft palate.

Vibrato - A more or less rapid fluctuation of tone, giving the effect of vibration, or throbbing. Most voices have a characteristic vibrato. Those in which there seems to be none are thought of as "straight."

Vital Capacity - Maximum breath which can be exhaled after forced inhalation; the total of all breath capacity.

Vocal Cords, Bands, Folds, Lips, Shelves, Wedges - The vibrating part of the larynx responsible for creating the initial vibration for tone.

Vocalises - Exercises specifically designed to strengthen and enhance the power, endurance and beauty of the vocal instrument.

Vocal Tract - The various organs and muscles of respiration, vibration, resonation and articulation that produce speech and singing.

Voice Box - The protective, bony outer covering of the vocal cords. Also known as the larynx.

Voiced Consonants - A speech sound that obstructs the flow of air and requires the vocal cords to vibrate, creating an accompanying tone.

Vowel - Voiced sound consisting of a single tone without consonant or articulator interference.

Vowel Modification - A slight, intentional adjustment to the sound of a vowel in the upper range, which produces a more rounded (or darkened) and pleasing tone.

Whisper - Completely breathy sound.

Wobble - A kind of vocal movement where the frequency of oscillation or pulsation of tone is too slow (as in a vibrato that is too slow).

Bibliography

ADLER, KURT (1976), The Art of Accompanying and Coaching. New York, New York: Da Capo Press.

APPELMAN, D. RALPH (1967), The Science of Vocal Pedagogy. Bloomington/London. Indiana University Press.

BENJAMIN, BEN E. (1978), Are You Tense?, New York: Pantheon.

BOTUME, FRANK J. (1987), Modern Singing Methods, Their Use and Abuse. New York: Oliver Ditson Company.

BRODNITZ, M.D., FRIEDRICH B. (1988), Keep Your Voice Healthy. Boston, Toronto: Little, Brown, & Co.

BROWER, HARRIETTE (1920), Vocal Mastery. New York, New York: Frederick A. Stokes Co.

BROWN, WILLIAM EARL (1973), Vocal Wisdom. Boston: Crescendo Publishing Company.

BURGIN, JOHN CARROLL (1973), Teaching Singing. Metuchen, New Jersey. The Scarecrow Press, Inc.

CHRISTY, VAN A. (1975), Foundations in Singing. Dubuque, Iowa: Wm. C. Brown Co. Publishers. (Catalog #BKBR05846)

COFFIN, BERTON (1987), Sounds of Singing. Metuchen, New Jersey and London, England: The Scarecrow Press, Inc.

COOPER, MORTON (1973), Modern Techniques of Vocal Rehabilitation. Springfield, Illinois: Charles C. Thomas.

FUCHS, VIKTOR (1964), The Art of Singing and Voice Technique. New York: London House and Maxwell.

GARCIA, MANUEL (1970). Hints On Singing. Canoga Park, California: Summit Publishing.

GOLDOVSKY, BORIS (1968), Bringing Opera To Life. Englewood, New Jersey: Prentice-Hall.

GRAY, HENRY, F.R.S., (1977), Gray's Anatomy, Bounty Books, New York.

HAMMAR, RUSSELL A. (1978). Singing - An Extension of Speech. Metuchen, N.J. & London; The Scarecrow Press, Inc.

HARPSTER, RICHARD W (1984), Technique in Singing. New York: Schirmer Books.

HERBERT-CAESARI, E. (1965), The Alchemy of Voice. London: Robert Hall Limited.

HERBERT-CAESARI, E. (1963), The Voice of the Mind. Boston: Crescendo Publishing Co.

HINES, JEROME (1982), Great Singers on Great Singing. New York: Proscenium Publishers.

JACOBI, HENRY N. (1982), Building Your Best Voice. Englewood Cliffs, New Jersey: Prentice-Hall.

JUDD, PERCY (1951), Vocal Technique. Great Britain: Sylvan Press.

KAGEN, SERGIUS (1950), On Study in Singing. New York, NY: Dover Publications.

KLEIN, JOSEPH J. (1967), Singing Technique. Princeton, New Jersey: D. Van Nostrand Co., Inc.

LAMPERTI, FRANCESCO, A Treatise on the Art of Singing. New York: Edward Schuberth & Co.

LAWSON, JAMES TERRY, M.D., (1955), Full-Throated Ease. Melville, N.Y.:Belwin Mills Publishing Co. by arrangement with Western Music Co. Ltd., Vancouver, B.C. Canada. (Catalog #90017)

LEHMANN, LILLI (1904), How To Sing. New York: The Macmillan Company.

LEYERLE, WILLIAM D., (1986), Vocal Development Through Organic Imagery. Genesee, New York: State University of New York, College of the Arts and Science.

LIDELL, LUCINDA (1984), The Book of Massage. New York: Simon & Shuster, Inc., A Fireside Book.

McCLOSKY, DAVID BLAIR (1972). Your Voice At Its Best. Boston, Mass: The Boston Music Co.

MANEN, LUCIE (1974), The Art of Singing. Bryn Mawr, Pa.: Theodore Presser Company.

MEANO, CARLO, M.D. (1967), The Human Voice in Speech and Song. Springfield, Illinois: Charles C. Thomas.

MORIARTY, JOHN (1975), Diction, Massachusetts: E.C. Schirmer Music Company.

MILLER, KENNETH E. (1990), Principles of Singing. Englewood Cliffs, New Jersey: Prentice-Hall.

MILLER, RICHARD (1977), English, French, German and Italian Techniques of Singing: A Study in National Tonal Preferences and How They Relate to Functional Efficiency. Metuchen, New Jersey: The Scarecrow Press, Inc.

MILLER, RICHARD (1986), The Structure of Singing. New York: Schirmer Books.

PROSCHOWLSKY (1923), The Way to Sing, Boston, MA: C.C. Birchard & Co.

PIERCE, ANNE E. & LIEBLING, ESTELLE (1937), Class Lessons in Singing. New York: Silver Burdett Company.

REID, CORNELIUS (1965), The Free Voice. New York: Coleman-Ross Company, Inc.

ROMA, LISA (1956), The Science and Art of Singing. New York: G. Schirmer, Inc.

ROSEWALL, RICHARD B. (1961), Handbook of Singing. Evanston, Illinois: Dickerson Press.

SABLE, BARBARA KINSEY (1982), The Vocal Sound. Englewood Cliffs, New Jersey: Prentice-Hall.

SCHIOTZ (1953), The Singer and His Art. New York/ London/ Evanston: Harper and Row Publishing.

SCHJEIDE, PH.D., OLE A. (1967), How to Avoid Vocal Trouble. Princeton, New Jersey/ Toronto/ London/ Melbourne: D. Van Nostrand Co., Inc.

SHAKESPEARE, WILLIAM (1893), The Art of Singing, Volume I. Boston, Mass., Oliver Ditson Co.

SHAKESPEARE, WILLIAM (1893), The Art of Singing, Volume 2. Boston, Mass., Oliver Ditson Co.

SIMPSON, JAMES B. (1988), Simpson's Contemporary Quotations, Boston/New York/London: Houghton Mifflin Co.

STANTON, ROYAL (1983), Steps to Singing for Voice Classes. Belmont, CA., Wadsworth Publishing Co.

TETRAZZINI, LUISA and ENRICO CARUSO, (1909), The Art of Singing. New York. Da Capo Press.

TETRAZZINI, LUISA (1923), How To Sing. New York. Da Capo Press.

TREE, CHARLES (1911), How to Acquire Ease of Voice Production. Boston, Mass: The Boston Music Co.

TRUSLER, IVAN & EHRET, WALTER, (1960). Functional Lessons In Singing. Englewood Cliffs, N.J.: Prentice-Hall.

VENNARD, WILLIAM (1967), Singing, the Mechanism and Technique. New York: Carl Fischer, Inc.

WALL, JOAN et al, (1990), Diction for Singers, Dallas: Pst... Inc.

WHITE, ERNEST G. (1950), Science and Singing, Boston, Mass.: Crescendo Publishing Corp.

WILSON, HARRY ROBERT (1959), Artistic Choral Singing. New York: G. Schirmer, Inc.

WITHERSPOON, HERBERT (1925), Singing, New York, New York: G. Schirmer, Inc.

Index

A

Adduct, 350
Alcoholic Beverages, 297-298
Allergies, 299
Alto, 266-277, 271, 308
Anchoring Tone, 88-91
Approximate, 350
Aria, 350
Arpeggio, 81, 202-204, 254, 350
Articulation, 316, 347, 350
Articulator, 242, 247, 346-348
Attack, 102, 209, 307, 317, 350

B

Back, 275
Baritone, 266, 268, 271, 308
Base, 275
Basic Vowels, 94-95
Bass, Basso, 266, 268, 271, 308
Beginning of a Yawn, 77-78, 156, 292, 308, 318
Belly, 309
Belly Breathing, 350
Belt, To Check Breathing, 113
Blend, 122-138
Blowing, 351
Break, 130, 141
Breast Bone, 351
Breath Control, 24-25, 29-30, 326-327
Breath Flow, 317

Breath Management, 351
Breath Support, 17, 24, 28-29, 324-325
Breath Support Muscle Group, 17, 324-325
Breathing System, 14-15, 24, 28-29,33
Breathwork, 314-320
Breathy, 308, 318
Bright, 42
Brilliance, 88

C

Catch Breath, 233
Chest, 338
Chest Resonance, 123-124
Clavicle, 352
Clavicular Breathing, 352
Clear, 151, 163, 186, 352
Colds, 295-296
Coloratura Soprano, 266-267
Colorature, 266-267
Compound Vowel, 94, 212-214
Consonant, 241-255
Consonant Modifications, 252-255
Constrictive Vowels, 94-95, 119
Contralto, 266-267, 271
Controlled Release Exercise, 29-31
Counterbalancing, 150-152
Covered, 317
Covering, 160
Crack, 43,129-134, 318

D

Dark Timbre, 353
Darkening Vowels, 160
Delayed Vowel, 212-215
Depressed Larynx, 161-162, 353
Depth, 88
Diaphragm, 17, 325-327
Diction, 320, 353
Diphthong, 94, 212-215
Dramatic Soprano, 267
Dramatic Tenor, 268
Dynamics, 174-175, 353

E

Ear, 40, 67-69, 266, 269
Edge, 343, 354
Emotion, 282, 354
Enunciation, 354
Exercise (Physical), 286-287
Exercise (vocal), 43-46, 112-116,
    174, 200
Exhalation, 30-31, 326
Expression, 6, 100, 136, 311

F

Falsetto, 122, 141-142
Floating Tone, 19
Floating Position (Larynx), 161-162
Floating Ribs, 354
Florid, 354
Flowing, 209-239
Focal Point, 64-65, 67, 71

Focus, 62, 124
Forced, 22, 55, 316-317
Forced Breathing, 355
Forward, 37-49, 66, 70, 127,136,
    246, 249, 306
Framework, 314-320

G

Glottis, 333-335
Great Scale, 170-172

H

Half-Voice, 355
Hard Palate, 66, 346-347
Head Voice/Resonance, 122-123
High, 355
High Larynx, 161-163
Hole-in-the-Wall, 64-65
Hum, 116-117, 251, 292

I

Imagery, 40, 318
Imaginary, half, or silent "H," 103-109
Indispensable Minimum, 21
Inner Ears, 68-71
Inner Smile, 52-53
Initiating Tone, 102-103
Intensity, 21, 79, 115, 149, 190, 204,
    210
Intercostals, 356

K

L

M

N

O

P

V

W

Y

There is a vitality, a life force, a quickening
that is translated through you into action,
and because there is only one of you in all time,
this expression is unique.

If you block it,
it will never exist through any other medium
and be lost.
The world will not have it.
It is not your business to determine how good it is;
nor how valuable it is;
nor how it compares with other expressions.
It is your business to keep it yours, clearly and directly,
to keep the channel open.

You do not have to believe in yourself or your work.
You have to keep open and aware directly
to the urges that motivate you.

Keep the channel open.
No artist is pleased.
There is no satisfaction whatever at any time.
There is only a queer, divine dissatisfaction;
a blessed unrest that keeps us marching
and makes us more alive than the others.

Martha Graham to Agnes DeMille